This book is dedicated to my friend Margie Jones…
From your best friend, the Lodging House Cat

SCOUSE, CHOPPERS
&
SPACE HOPPERS

SCOUSE, CHOPPERS
&
SPACE HOPPERS

Happy Days and Hard Times in Sixties
and Seventies Liverpool

CRISSY ROCK

JOHN BLAKE

Published by John Blake Publishing,
2.25, The Plaza,
535 Kings Road,
Chelsea Harbour,
London SW10 0SZ

www.johnblakebooks.com

www.facebook.com/johnblakebooks ▪
twitter.com/jblakebooks ▪

First published in paperback in 2018

ISBN: 978 1 78606 950 4

British Library Cataloguing-in-Publication Data:

A catalogue record for this book is available from the British Library.

Design by www.envydesign.co.uk

Printed and bound in Great Britain by Clays Ltd, Elcograf S.p.A.

1 3 5 7 9 10 8 6 4 2

Papers used by John Blake Publishing are natural, recyclable products made from
wood grown in sustainable forests. The manufacturing processes conform to the
environmental regulations of the country of origin.

Every reasonable effort has been made to trace copyright-holders of material reproduced
in this book, but if any have been inadvertently overlooked the publishers would be
glad to hear from them.

John Blake Publishing is an imprint of Bonnier Books UK
www.bonnierbooks.co.uk

CONTENTS

FOREWORD

I have known Crissy Rock for a long, long time. I knew her at what was probably the lowest ebb of her life. She had been knocked from pillar to post and had been in terrible, abusive relationships yet she always seemed to bounce back smiling. Only those of us who knew Crissy well realised what a terrible struggle she had been through, and neither she nor I will speak of them here. But I think her life changed for the better after a meeting I happened to arrange for her.

I had a small casting agency in Liverpool and previously had the privilege to meet and work with Ken Loach (in my opinion, the greatest film director of his time) in two of his films, *Riff-Raff* and *Raining Stones*. Anyway, one day, I had a phone call from him. He told me he was making a film, called *Ladybird Ladybird*, about a young woman who had been through the mill, both physically and mentally. He told me he had auditioned dozens of women, but none of them seemed right for the part. I obviously thought of Crissy, and arranged for Ken to come to Liverpool to audition her in a local club with a few others. After interviewing them, he told me he couldn't make his mind up. He especially liked two of them very much, one of them being Crissy. He knew he had to make a decision soon as shooting was to start right away. As seemed fated, he chose Crissy. How could he not?

Anyway, the film was made and it became an international success. Crissy won many awards for her fantastic performance. This success opened doors for her into many more acting roles, notably the fantastic *Benidorm*. Her career as a comedienne and actress has taken her to many places, but she's never forgotten where she came from – Liverpool, the city I've lived in most of my life.

This memoir of growing up in Liverpool is a great tribute to a magic city, and her love for the place – through good times and bad – comes out of every page. I love Crissy for coming through all her heartache with smiles, humour and the stories to show for it. She is no doubt the best comedienne on the circuit – plus she's the first to volunteer for charity shows and does everything to give back to her home town.

I loved reading this trip down memory lane, as Crissy takes you by the hand and guides you through one of the best cities in the world, through some of its most brilliant years. For those that weren't there for it all, I hope you enjoy the ride. And for those that were, I hope you can relive some of it for yourself – I know I did.

Ricky Tomlinson

INTRODUCTION

Back in the 1970s they used to have an advert on the TV that went something like this, 'Hello, my name is Victor Kiam. I used a razor that I liked so much I bought the company.' Well, my name's Crissy. I wrote a book once, and people liked it so much they wanted another one. And here it is, but with a difference: this book is about history. Not the type of history you Google, look up on Wikipedia, or were forced to listen to in school from some plaid-shirt-wearing teacher with BO, who was always screaming down your neck. Nah, this history is gonna be interesting because it's from my perspective of Liverpool in the 1960s and 70s. Now, don't be huffing and puffing and saying you already know all there is to know about Liverpool at that time just because you once bought a bootleg copy of The Beatles' *White Album*. The history I'm going to tell you covers one of the most amazing times for the city and the most amazing time to be alive.

So, proceed with caution – which is a nice way of saying there might be one or two swear words laced throughout the chapters that follow. Nothing too bad, of course, but nothing you'd want to read to your kids at bedtime. Well, I suppose if you grow up in a so-called ghetto in any city in Britain you're gonna end up with a colourful turn of phrase. I grew up in Liverpool's ghetto so my phrase is in 3D Technicolor super surround sound. Anyhow, you've been warned. And if you're expecting a uniform timeline, a year-to-year, month-to-month ordered recollection of those two precious decades, then don't. The sixties and seventies were entirely unorganised and so are my memories of them. So, get yourself a cup of tea, snuggle into your settee, and prepare to be flung backwards and forwards through the sixties and seventies with my mishmash memories of the great city of Liverpool.

Liverpool is the third most-visited city in the world, according to the *Rough Guides* book. Or at least it was in 2014 when my friend heard them mention it on the *Ten O'Clock News*. Now, don't be shaking your head with disbelief; if my friend said she heard it on the *Ten O'Clock News* then she did, as she's the type of Catholic who believes she'll spontaneously combust if she tells a lie. Liverpool city is – or was – the third most-visited city on the planet straight after Sarajevo in second place, and Rio de Janeiro in first. I personally thought Sarajevo was unlikely, but if my self-flagellating Catholic friend said it's gospel, then it's gospel. Anyway, Liverpool wasn't always one of the most popular destinations in the world. In fact, there was a time when you only visited the city if you liked rubble or docks as Liverpool was Hitler's second favourite city to bomb the crap out of, and he left most of it in bits. The docks were so famous the city was once called the second city of the Empire, and Europe's New York too.

But that's all ancient history and what we're here to talk about is 'my' Liverpool, the Liverpool that gave birth to The Beatles, comedy legends such as Ken Dodd and Jimmy Tarbuck, and a pan of stew whose name became synonymous with the people who live here; people who, I think, are the warmest and funniest people you could ever wish to meet.

I mentioned a pan of stew, which probably confused the hell out of one or two readers who aren't that clued up about the city (didn't buy the *White Album*). Well, the stew in question is Scouse, as in Scouser, or person who was born in Liverpool. Scouse was taken from the word 'lobscouse', which was a stew eaten by Norwegian sailors. My nan used to say that the nineteenth-century sailors gave Scouse to people from the poorest parts of the city, who'd head for the docks whenever the Norwegians came into shore. Scouse was a dead cheap dish made up of all kinds of vegetable odds and ends and any kind of meat or fish that was handy. For us as kids, it was something we'd eat regularly, although nowadays it seems to be a meal that's only really eaten for the nostalgia of it, or if you're a tourist. They reckon that the name truly stuck as a term for the people of the city not because of the stew, but because of the late great Warren Mitchell in his iconic role as Alf Garnett in the BBC TV sitcom *Till Death Us Do Part*. He was forever calling his daughter's layabout Liverpudlian husband a 'Scouse git'!

Now, before I stop waffling on and let you actually get into reading this book, I'd like to add one final note; whether they call themselves Liverpudlians, Scousers, or just plain scallies, it's the people of Liverpool who have made this – the city I love – into the most welcoming and unforgettable place I could ever wish to call my home.

Crissy Rock

CHAPTER ONE

'ANY OL' RAGS!'

'**R**ags… Any ol' rags!' Billy's voice bellowed out across the square, echoing through the arches of Windsor Gardens, the tenement block where I lived with my nan, mam and dad till the age of thirteen. Billy was the ragman who tirelessly pushed his cart through the streets of Liverpool 8, in the south end of the city, and the surrounding areas. Whenever he came to our block, me and the other kids would appear from all directions and leg it over to his cart with the bits of clothing we had to trade. I remember him clearly – standing there with his broad toothless smile and his legs astride like he was the Pied Piper of Rags.

We always exchanged our old wares with Billy, but only those that weren't good enough for the pawn shop. In return, we got to look in Billy's big bag that was slung over his barrow handles, to choose either a balloon or a bird on a wire. Of course this wasn't a real bird, not like our budgie Joey. Nah, this bird was plastic and stuck on a piece of wire attached to a stick, which, when you swung it around, made a loud whistling noise. If you didn't fancy a balloon or a whistling bird, or if the kids before you had already got the last of them, then you could choose either a cup and saucer or a patterned plate.

Sometimes Billy would have little goldfish in plastic bags filled with water and all the neighbourhood kids would fight over them. The goldfish were easily my favourites, and although we didn't have a goldfish bowl, when I finally did get a goldfish, I stuck mine in a scrubbed-out jam jar. I felt a kind of peace and joy watching that little fish swimming round and round in its jar. However, my joy was short-lived when the next day I discovered it floating lifeless on top of the water. I remember running to Nan – who was in the back kitchen, washing dishes – crying to her that my goldfish wasn't swimming any more. She calmly dried her hands on her pinny and said to me, 'You daft bugger! The fish is asleep, that's all. It's knackered from swimming around the jam jar all night.' At the time, I supposed Nan was right as my eyes were totally knackered from just watching the fish swim. Nan picked up the jam jar and said, 'Come on, let's put it to bed!' I followed her to the bathroom and watched as she poured the fish and the water straight down the toilet pan. She flushed the chain. 'There,' she said. And that was that.

I still can't believe I spent the rest of that day and half the night staring down the toilet pan, waiting for my goldfish to have a Lazarus moment and swim up from the U-bend! I learnt a lesson that day – no more dodgy goldfish off our ragman. From then on I'd settle for a balloon or, better still, a plazzy friggin' bird on a wire.

Our good clothes (not that we had many) never went to Billy, they were destined for the pawn shop on Crown Street. The front of the shop had lots of things in its window, all kinds of oddments; the flotsam and jetsam people unloaded for cash when times got hard. Over the door there were three big balls. Nan said those three balls meant 'two-to-one you won't get your stuff back'. She would often send me to the pawn shop. She'd place coats, cardigans, hats and any other bits of clothing in the middle of her tablecloth, pull up the four corners, then tie them tight over the bundle. 'Go and take them to the pawn shop for us,' she'd say, with a strict warning not to accept less than ten bob (fifty pence) for the lot. As I picked the bundle up, she would add, 'And don't let anyone see you go in!' See me go in? You could spot me from Birkenhead, the size of the bundle I was carrying!

In those days everything got pawned. The pawn shops would take anything from a wooden leg to a blanket, even sets of false teeth. I remember my grandad being in Newsham Park Hospital and saying, 'I can't eat this dinner coz your nan's forgotten to bring me bloody-well teeth!' And every time she visited, he'd ask Nan to bring his false teeth in and she kept putting him off, saying, 'I can't remember where you put them, Joe.' That was because she'd pawned them and didn't have the money to get them back out! So Grandad had to suck his spuds all the time he was in there.

When I wasn't off to the pawn shop for Nan, I would be in Ali's, the corner shop, where I would hand him a note so I could buy our groceries on tick, or the 'never-never' as people called it. And when all my chores were done and dusted, it was off out to play and oh, what a playground we had! Sixties Liverpool was full of tenement blocks and pre-war concrete buildings, the ideal place for us kids to play, build dens…and get injured. Large houses that once belonged to the Victorian ruling classes were now showing the signs of wear and tear, or as Nan used to say, 'Their posh clothes were crumbling, revealing their dirty vests and grimy pants'. It would be another forty-odd years before the powers that be realised what they had and got round to rescuing those amazing houses although in the end they only bothered rescuing those houses in the city centre, most of the other areas got flattened.

Upper Parliament Street ran along the back of Windsor Gardens, and just up from there was Granby Street. Granby was alive…always! The beating heart of Liverpool 8, it thrived with shops and people of all colours, who sold clothes and food from every possible place you might see in a school atlas. Music of all kinds cut through the air from morning till night and the smells of exotic spices tickled your nose, making you sneeze or salivate. It truly was a beautiful melting pot of cultures. Along Granby Street was the Post Office, then the chandler's shop, an Aladdin's cave where the smell of carbolic soap hung in the air. The shop that sold paraffin was next, and then the police station (that never seemed to be open). Then, if you kept walking, you would come across the men who played Pigeon Toss (Pitch-and-Toss). These men were mostly from the Caribbean and always seemed to be shouting out loud, or laughing out loud, or both.

Exiting the top of Granby Street took you onto Princes Road (or Princes Avenue) – depending on whether you thought you were posh or not. Turn left onto Princes and you would be greeted by the ornate Sunburst Gates of Princes Park, designed by Joseph Paxton, the same fella who designed the Crystal Palace in London.

Princes was the first of three parks – the other two being Sefton, and Otterspool – that were next to each other. The three parks were right smack on our doorstep. Well, maybe not right smack on it, not unless our doorstep was a mile-and-a-half long. But they were close enough for me to go play in without having to be chaperoned by my mam or dad. Princes, or 'Prinny Park' as we called it, was the first park you came to if you were heading up from the city centre and it's where most of us played in the summer. I remember walking down the tree-lined leafy drive, heading deep into the park towards the gravestone of Judy the donkey, dated 1926. For twenty-one years this donkey had delighted thousands of Edwardian kids by giving rides around the park. No matter how many times I saw that gravestone I always felt a little pang of sadness.

Prinny's Serpentine boating lake was perfect for catching fish with just a piece of thread and a bent pin with an unfortunate worm impaled on its end. However, you would have to make sure you didn't disturb the 'serious' fishermen who sat there all day long (catching sod-all), or else they'd give you a kick and tell you to eff off. And back then they could get away with hitting us kids if we were being annoying little shits. I remember whenever lads from the Dingle saw us fishing, they'd call me and me mates tomboys, or the extreme of. But whoever said girls couldn't fish, hey?

Princes Park had a playground area with swings and slides and a roundabout you would risk life and limb to go on. As soon as you jumped on, that one lunatic mate would always get carried away and spin the thing like she was trying to make it take off. It was at that moment you realised maybe jumping on wasn't a great idea as now you couldn't get back off without having to do a face plant into the gravel, or a James Bond stunt roll into a nettle bush. I'd always opt for clinging on for dear life, hoping that by the time it did slow down, my lunch was still inside my stomach! The sandpit was great because we only ever got to see sand at New Brighton Beach and my mam only ever took us there now and again. So, moulding gravelly sand into our version of castles was the next best thing to building proper sandcastles in New Brighton. Those were the days before poop bags so when you dived into the sandpit, you stood the risk of getting a face decorated with dog poo, which was sure to put a damper on your day.

I loved Princes Park. When we weren't fishing for tiddlers or wiping sandy poo off our clothes and faces, a gang of us would just go and sit on the grass with our jam butties, supping water that had sherbet in for flavour. The days were warm and long and we'd run about playing Tick, (the Scouse name for the game 'Tag') or my mate Maureen Gee, or Cathleen Disley and her sisters, Donna and Colette, would pick daisies and make daisy-chain necklaces, then hold buttercups under our chins to see if we liked butter – although we didn't really know what butter was as most of the time we used dripping from the oven pan to spread on our bread.

Sefton Park was beautiful, with its ponds and its huge boating lake surrounded by black and white boat huts that resembled midget Tudor houses. The lake was where I got to see my first ever swans. I remember being gobsmacked at how serene they looked compared to all the other ducks I'd seen before, almost like they were the duck royal family or something. But then I went near one of their chicks and they suddenly lost their serenity and came at me like a bunch of bleedin' skinheads, chasing me up a grass-bank and halfway along a path until they got bored and went back to looking like butter wouldn't melt in their beaks. The Palm House stood out on a visit to Sefton; like the kind of building you only ever saw on the documentaries of the day, which were in black and white on our telly and usually faded, crooked and requiring fifteen twists of a TV top aerial if you wanted to see them at all. We used to march up to the big glass doors and quickly dodge inside to see all the tropical plants, some of which reached right up to the domed glass roof. Two minutes later, we'd come bursting back out, sweating and gasping for air because of the tropical humidity.

There was an aviary in Sefton Park too. This meant us little scallywags not only got to see tropical plants but we also got to see exotic birds from lots of places around the world too – places with impossible-to-pronounce names. Actually, most of the names were impossible to read, so the birds could have been from friggin' Widnes for all we knew! I was always in awe of the colours of the birds and the sounds they made, a million miles away from the cooing of the scally pigeons I'd grown used to dodging in case they dropped a load on me. I think I always felt a bit sorry for the birds in the aviary. They were meant to be in Africa, or India, or friggin' Outer Mongolia…anywhere but a manmade park in the middle of Liverpool.

Otterspool – the third park – was the 'now-and-then park', as you only visited it now and then because it was at the arse end of Sefton Park and a good hour's walk from home if you were dragging your feet. But Otterspool had the woods to play in, and what kid doesn't like woods? The swing was the highlight of Otterspool woods. Made from bits of old rope twisted and knotted together, with a half-tree branch for a seat, it was located at the top of a steep clay hill that might as well have been a mountain for the struggle you had trying to climb to the top of it. The swing itself pushed off from the hilltop and swung out to a trouser-filling thirty feet above a Tarmac path. It was safe-ish on the way out, but once you swung back, your friends would jump on with you. Then more and more kids would join in until it looked less like a swing and more like a human wrecking ball, with the day's casualties slowly losing their grip, one by one, and hopefully landing on a bush instead of the blacktop. Half the time you didn't even know the kids who were clinging to your clothes for dear life while their pissy crotches were being pressed up against your face.

The promenade in Otterspool overlooked the River Mersey and had a long grass verge that ran the length of it, with old York stone seats dotted about here and there. Some of the seats were surrounded by thick hedges that were probably meant for courting couples to have a sneaky snog! I was happy just to sit there, snogless, in my own private little world, looking across the Mersey to the distant mountains of Wales. There were always flowers in Otterspool, lots of different types I'd take home and make perfume from, usually by boiling up a cup of water, cramming the flowers into it, then adding the secret ingredient (a splash of my dad's Brut aftershave). I remember being completely chuffed with myself that I'd made my own real perfume that smelled absolutely gorgeous. It actually smelled like crap, like crushed flower stems tinged with Brut, but when you're a little kid you tend to big up your achievements. After a long happy day of botanical suffocation, death by swing, and poo-smeared faces, our stomachs would start to rumble, signalling it was time to head off home, like a conga line of little ragamuffins.

On the days that were so sweltering hot we couldn't be bothered going to the park, we would always find things to entertain ourselves. The tar on the road was a fun distraction, rising like bubbles of black chewing gum; you could literally spend hours prodding those bubbles with a stick and never get bored, while waiting your turn to swing on a bit of rope someone had strung to the lamppost. Back then, the days were filled with an endless choice of free games: Kick the Can, Hopscotch, Tick, Simon Says, Lucy Locket and Rounders, to name but a few. There was no such thing as tablets, video games or mobile phone apps to sit all alone in your bedroom and be a boring bastard with, just good physical fun where you had to use your imagination.

Even on freezing cold days you would still play out if your mates came knocking. I'd bolt out of our front door, balaclava pulled over my head and a pair of mittens my mam knitted. Although I use the word 'knitted' in its loosest sense as she couldn't knit to save her life – hence the mittens looking like deformed cow udders and the face hole in the balaclava being so small, only one eye could peek through at a time! And although the bitter cold stung any exposed skin with a vengeance, and our wellington boots rubbed and chafed our legs as if their only goal in life was to give us severe welly-rash, us urban soldiers would stay out playing until the last bit of daylight was blotted from the winter sky. Then it was time to head off home, toes and fingers red raw and completely frozen, to the sound of your mam's echoing calls.

Pocket money was non-existent back then, unless you ran errands for a neighbour. Any money I did make would be spent on the *Bunty*, a well-known girls' comic of the time. Even though I couldn't read, I would make up my own stories as to what I thought the pictures were all about. The *Bunty* was great because the back page featured a cut-out doll. It also had cut-out paper clothes with tabs you could fold over to place the clothes on the doll. I used to mix and match the clothes and imagine I was that paper doll, all pretty and tall like some of me mates, the ones who always had the boys chasing after them. Sometimes I'd get sad because none of the boys liked me – well, they did, but not in the way they liked me mates. Nan used to say, 'Never mind, love. For every pan there's a lid.' It took me years to realise I was a wok!

Most of my friends had older sisters so they had a good choice of hand-me-downs they could borrow that always made them look smart and glamorous. I had four brothers, so I had all the balaclavas, welly boots and grey socks I could handle. The grey socks were the worst as they were what the boys wore for school. Every girl – except me – wore white socks to school. I couldn't even say my socks were stained in the wash because no one had a friggin' washing machine! Eventually, I stopped trying to be pretty, but I got fed up hanging round on my own while me mates paired off with lads. So I became the funny one, and me mates loved it. They used to laugh their heads off and say I should be on the stage. 'Yeah,' I'd say, 'the *landing* stage!'

I remember staying in one night to watch *I Love Lucy* on the telly. And oh, was Lucille Ball funny! I loved watching her so much that on those nights, I'd head off into the hallway and create my own little comedy shows. At first I would mimic what Lucy did but, later, I would start making up my own jokes and performances. I suppose I felt a sort of affinity with Lucy, because no matter how many times she got things wrong, she always smiled and carried on trying. Also, she was glamour-less. I don't mean she was ugly, far from it, but back then almost every Hollywood movie was filled with handsome men and glamorous women, and I never ever felt glamorous myself. Lucy was gorgeous, but she didn't shy away from pulling grotesque faces and falling into the most unglamorous situations possible. So I, like Lucy, followed the slapstick. The un-glamorous. The *I don't give a shit!* And whenever I couldn't play out because it was too dark, our hallway became my comedy theatre, and the coats that hung in our hallway became my audience. I'd be like, 'Good evening, everybody!' and I'd hold a colour torch up to my face to vary the faces I pulled and alter the atmosphere. Sometimes Nan would shout, 'Shurrup!' from the living room if I sang too loud or did a clomping dance, probably because the woman who lived below us would start banging the crap out of her ceiling with a brush pole. I always wondered how many holes and plaster cracks that annoying downstairs neighbour must have made in her ceiling, and what would happen if they all joined together: would the ceiling fall and squash her? Whenever Nan did shout, I'd whisper to my captivated coat audience, 'Hush, we have to be quiet now, because it's late and we're in the dark.' I bet you Lucille Ball wouldn't have put up with a banging neighbour and a complaining nan disturbing her coat performance. Anyway, most of my very appreciative coat audience ended up on Billy's rag cart.

'ANY OL' RAGS!'

I often wonder what became of Billy, that larger-than-life ragman whose voice bellowed through our tenement block, and who filled up our lives once a week with his plazzy birds on sticks, his half-dead goldfishes, and his patterned plates, cups and saucers. I can still see him in my mind's eye, checking over the rags we gave him. With his rough, reddened hands, his trousers always at half-mast up his legs, his overcoat two sizes too big, and most of all, his broad, toothless smile.

CHAPTER TWO

MOPTOPS, FURY AND GENTLEMAN JIM

I don't remember much of 1960; after all, I was only two years old. I suppose the most notable event is also the most obvious, that a certain Liverpool band started playing gigs in Hamburg, Germany, for the very first time. They performed under the name The Beatals – it probably sounded that way because it was the Germans that were saying the name in pidgin English and almost destroying what was to become one of the most iconic names in music history. The band changed their name to The Beatles, a name that at first seemed to bring them rotten luck, seeing as one of them was deported from Germany for being too young, another left the band, and two got arrested for setting fire to a condom – and before you say it, it wasn't a friction fire. Hamburg was also the place where the lads got their famous moptop haircuts, as influenced by a photographer called Astrid Kirchherr. I'd have loved to have been there to see the four lads sitting in a German barber shop, saying, 'Hey, Fritz, could you give us a cut'n'moptop?' And the barber replying, 'Ja, and vud you like something for dur veekend? To set on fire maybe?' Okay, that's my last attempt at a German accent.

The Beatles had gone to Germany because they'd grown weary of Liverpool. They told their manager Allan Williams that Liverpool had gotten pockmarked and couldn't compare to Hamburg. The 'Reeperbahn' (a piss-up entertainment district in Hamburg) was always open, while Liverpool was most definitely shut, boarded up, and laid to rest. Maybe they thought that way because the city was still a bombed-out wreck from the Blitz and waiting to be reborn into its glory days? Or perhaps they were reacting with the same frustration every struggling creative does when they're not getting the recognition they feel they deserve off the people who should be supporting them most? As the old saying goes, 'A prophet is never recognised in his own land'. It's funny to think that the Mersey beat was born not in Liverpool, like I used to think it was, but in Hamburg, Germany, albeit courtesy of four floppy-headed Scousers.

So, after slagging Liverpool off, The Beatles and their floppy hairdos came home and immediately struck a chord with the young clubgoers. They started to get lots of attention while filling out the lunchtime gigs they were performing at the Cavern Club. The Cavern, on the now world-famous Mathew Street, stood around the corner from a record store called NEMS, where you could stand in a soundproof booth, listening to the latest songs topping the charts.

NEMS stood for the North End Music Stores, which was once an old family furniture store that also sold drums, guitars and other types of musical instruments. It was the place to go if you wanted the very latest records and info on records due to be released. NEMS was the place where the entrepreneur Brian Epstein first dipped his toe in the music world when he joined the family business and started running the part of the store that sold records. The Beatles were always in the store, listening to the songs that were topping the charts; songs that were their direct competition.

Five years later, NEMS became the place me and my schoolgirl mates would invade whenever we'd play hooky from school. The store assistants were used to kids hanging around being little pains in the arse. I remember running up to the assistant, all excited and out of breath, asking, 'What's in the charts now?' The assistant would always point to a list that was on the counter, but because I could hardly read, I'd just randomly point and say, 'Is that one any good?' Then, changing my mind, 'Or that one? Is that one better?' The assistant would glare at me and the mob of mates standing behind me like our goal in life was to fuck up her day. But good enough, and like a pro, she would still play whatever song was topping the charts, then sigh as me and me mates piled into the nearest available booth to listen to it.

I can imagine what we must have looked like from outside the booth, all squashed together, while trying to wriggle our hips and dance. After a while, one of us was delegated to go back to the assistant and say, 'I don't like that record, can I hear the other one you said?' This time the assistant would lose it, turning red-faced and huffing like a big kid about to have a strop. Two records in, the assistant would get wise to the fact that we were skint and weren't serious customers at all. At this point the assistant would finally toss her toys out of the pram and chuck us out of the store. Sometimes we weren't even being a pain and had money to buy records, yet we'd still get kicked out because there was someone waiting to use the booth who had a lot more money than us. But for the most part we were chased out because we used to try singing half in and half out of the record booth, sounding like strangled goats and disturbing everyone else in the store.

I suppose it was only fair, us being ejected, as this was the main record store in Liverpool and at the time it was run by Brian Epstein himself. NEMS was where Brian first got to know The Beatles after attending one of their lunchtime gigs at the Cavern Club, just a few hundred yards from the store. They say he first offered to pay them £50 a week for life, which would be around £1,000 nowadays. But The Beatles were Scousers, so they immediately told him where to stick his offer. The next offer must have been a good one as he signed The Beatles on 1 October 1961 without a fuss. Although he was young and posh and these lads were different to anything he had ever seen or heard before, Brian still sussed that The Beatles had a magical something.

Imagine being there at the very beginning in that crowded, sweaty little Cavern Club, watching a four-lad band play to a local audience without the slightest clue as to how big they were gonna become right across the globe, and just what a massive influence they were gonna have on millions of future musicians right up to this day. I can't believe I was around at the time and had no friggin' interest in trying to get an autograph off the lads as they were leaving the Cavern…what a tit!

My favourite singer back then, who I listened to a lot more than I did The Beatles, was Billy Fury. Home grown, he was a Scouser like The Beatles and, like Ringo Starr, was born in the Dingle. To me, Billy Fury was tougher-looking than all of The Beatles put together, and his name was also about the coolest name any singer had at the time (even though I found out later that his real name was Ronald Wycherley).

I must have been six or seven when I noticed his singing for the first time and I started listening to all of his back tracks and older hits. He had something like twenty-four hits altogether, the same number as The Beatles, but he was never once able to get to the top of the charts with a No.1 hit. How unfair is that? He's got to have pissed someone off! Maybe some chief executive in the music industry who decided, 'Right, Fury! You're never getting a No.1 hit because you bonked my daughter!' You get what I mean. Billy used to sing rock 'n' roll, pop music and sometimes rhythm and blues too, but I didn't mind what type of music he sang, because it all sounded good.

As I mentioned, I started listening to him in the mid-sixties and so I had to seek out his earlier music as he'd been going since the fifties. I didn't have any records of his, but NEMS did, and whenever me and me mates invaded the shop, I would insist on listening to at least one Billy Fury song while we were there. Billy was so handsome and always gave off that troubled James Dean *Rebel Without a Cause* look. He could move too, like Elvis on steroids. He used to swivel his hips and make girls scream like old Spring-Heeled Jack (of more later) was on them.

I liked that Liverpool had worldwide superstars who grew up not even a ten-minute bus ride from where we lived. I could walk through town or sit on a park bench and think to myself that Billy, John, Paul, George, or Ringo might have walked through this part of town or parked their superstar arses on this park bench. My absolute favourite Billy Fury songs were 'Halfway to Paradise', 'Unchain My Heart' and 'It's Only Make Believe'. My favourite films of his were *Play It Cool* – a bit of an Elvis movie rip-off, but I loved it anyway – and of course, *That'll Be the Day*, in which he played my best ever gorgeous-guy role of rock singer Stormy Tempest. Nowadays, if you had someone in a movie called Stormy Tempest, it would probably be a woman and the film would be XXX-rated.

That'll Be the Day was one of the first movies I went to see as a teenager because I didn't really bother with the cinema that much, as me mates would only go when their boyfriends were paying, but when I heard there was a new film out and it had Billy Fury and my more recent heart-throb David Essex starring in it as the lead character, Jim MacLaine, then it was a no-brainer that I would be front-and-centre, third row from the back, which was my best seat. I remember the friends that I still hung around with from school days all laughing because they couldn't believe that I was still hooked on all things Billy

Fury. That film was the best film I'd ever seen up to that time, and after watching it even my friends thought the same, but I did find myself leaning more towards fancying David Essex as the film went on.

My nan didn't like The Beatles, Billy Fury, or David Essex – they weren't of her generation. In fact, she'd barely got into Elvis when he became famous. Nan's pride and joy was a radiogram which sat under the window like a coffin, and was reserved for the playing of Jim Reeves' records only. Billy Fury and The Beatles were certainly a far cry from 'Gentleman Jim Reeves' as he was known, and other singers like Connie Francis and yodelling Slim Whitman. 'Welcome to My World' was Nan's favourite song, closely followed by 'He'll Have to Go', and then 'Distant Drums'. To be honest, I loved those songs as well because I'd become so used to hearing them. More often than not, as I arrived home from school, 'Welcome to My World' would be playing on the radiogram. As I came through the door, Nan would always have a smile for me. I can still hear her now, saying, 'Hello, me little one. D'you wanna join me in a dance?' I'd always smile and nod, then run over to where she stood, grinning with her arms wide open. I would step onto her slippers and let her waltz me round the room, singing along word-perfect to the record. I'd squeal with laughter as she closed her eyes and lost herself in her dreams.

My nan used to go mad whenever we'd listen to The Beatles on her radiogram: 'Turn that off!' she'd say, 'And stop shaking your head or it's gonna fall off! You'll end up with meningitis, shaking your head like that!' Later, when the Fab Four got even more famous, we used to wear the plastic wigs that made you look like John Lennon or Paul McCartney, and we'd dance around the living room like loons. In truth, the plastic wigs made you look nothing like John or Paul at all, but if you jumped about enough, sang 'oooh' and shook your head to the meningitis-getting stage then your mates might just guess who the fuck you were supposed to be! The plastic wigs didn't half used to scrape the back of your neck, and they'd give you a rash that my nan would always notice: 'You've been wearing those stupid things again and shaking your head to those devil songs!' I swear Nan's only regular conversation in the mid-sixties was about us shaking our heads.

For those Scousers who didn't have a major gripe with anything Beatles-related, music played a large part in their lives. Just walk past any house in and around the city in those days and you'd hear the new generation of music being blasted from radiograms and record players, and from the doorways of the pubs that were on almost every street corner. Fury, The Beatles, Cilla Black, Adam Faith and Mr Squeaky Clean himself, Cliff Richard, made our days brighter and our nights wilder, but my nan always stayed faithful to her Gentleman Jim.

In July 1964, a newsflash came on my nan's radiogram, announcing that Jim Reeves had died in a plane crash. Nan dropped the dishes she was drying, fell to her knees and sobbed her heart out.

CHAPTER THREE

THE WALLS CAME TUMBLIN' DOWN

Dorothy, in *The Wizard of Oz*, closed her eyes and said, 'There's no place like home.' And she was right because for most of the children of my generation there really was no place like home. It was the early 1960s and not one of us had a pet horse down at the stables. Our parents didn't have a nice little car they were paying off on the finance. There were no holiday homes, villas in Spain, all-inclusive holidays to the Caribbean, or Christmas shopping trips to New York. For most of us kids a couple of rainy days at Butlins or Pontins holiday camps were all we had to look forward to, and believe me, we did look forward to them.

Back then newly-wed couples often had to live with parents until they had enough money to buy furniture for a place of their own. My mam and dad were no different and had moved in with my nan in her flat in 11d Windsor Gardens while there was still wedding confetti on their heads. We appreciated a lot more in those days because we didn't have a lot. The heart of the family really was your home – freezing in winter, far too hot in summer and damp the whole year round. Most houses never had a proper bath, just a tin one you dragged in from the yard and stuck in front of the fire to get a scrub in once a week on a Sunday. There was a Victorian swimming baths on Lodge Lane (at the top of Upper Parliament Street) that got most of its custom, not from people swimming, but from the public baths where you could get a hot bath and a small bar of soap for threepence.

The old houses had toilets in the back yard that were called outhouses, if you were a bit posh. We were anything but posh so we just called them the 'outside loo' or the 'back-bog'. There was always a Jerry bucket stuck in the room for those cold winter nights when going to the outside toilet meant taking your life in your hands. There was no toilet paper – well, not any particular paper used for that job only. What we did have was a newspaper ripped into squares. This meant that most people spent the day walking round with newsprint on their arses! Your bedroom was your living room, your kitchen, and sometimes even your toilet. And you had to share a bed too. In our house there were that many people in the bed I didn't know what it was like to sleep on my own till I got married.

But I loved my home in Windsor Gardens more than I can say, so I understood the sorrow felt by those who lived in the L8 area of Liverpool, whose houses were being condemned and torn down. Those of us born in the city at that time were the last in our generation to be born into the old Liverpool, and now we watched as it all came tumbling down to make way for the Liverpool we know today. The old Liverpool 8 had grown tired and fallen into disarray. All of the houses that were said to be beyond repair were being pulled down. However, the council had stopped doing repairs on the old houses a long time before that, and up to 80,000 properties had become unfit to live in.

It's strange to think now that in the beginning most people were happy about the regeneration. They'd heard the propaganda, the wonderful stories describing how regeneration was a good thing, a new hope that would result in them having houses of the future: houses with bathrooms, inside toilets, houses that were fresh and free of damp. How could they have known their communities were about to be broken up and left devastated, the same communities that were the life and breath of Liverpool? Everyone knew everyone, families grew up together, generation after generation watching out for, and taking care of each other. Regeneration was about to take all of this away. Within a few short years the council succeeded in doing more damage to those Liverpool communities than Hitler and his German Fokker planes ever did.

The first sign of change was when the cranes with the big wrecking balls rumbled on to Upper Parliament and Granby Street, smashing to pieces not just the houses, but the communities that made Liverpool such a warm and welcoming city. Then the bulldozers and the tipper trucks came in and the old Liverpool started tumbling down. Liverpool 8 looked like a war zone: mountains of bricks, glass everywhere, massive beams of wood being constantly burnt and causing the air to smell like every night was Bonfire Night. I remember seeing elderly men and women almost crying, looking lost and bewildered as they were forced to relocate to the outskirts of Liverpool, to streets and areas half of them had never even heard of.

Swainbanks removal vans zipped here and there, hired by those who could afford a proper removal service. For others there was the milkman with his cart, who was always up for earning an extra few bob, cash in hand. But for the majority of those leaving their homes, furniture was carried, heaped onto a pram, or stuck on the back of borrowed carts.

Yet for us kids who didn't understand what our parents were going through – being forced to witness the destruction of all they'd known – the debris and the empty properties left by the slum clearance became an action playground; venues for adventure with limitless opportunities to play for hours on end. For all the local government's efforts to have the buildings 'tinned up' immediately after being vacated in order to stop children, vandals and thieves getting at them, this was never an obstacle for long. Us kids had a field day playing war on the rubble of half-demolished houses. How none of us were killed, God only knows.

At the time, getting up in our house was a case of first-up, best-dressed. Luckily for me, I only had brothers so unless one of them wanted to wear my skirts, I was sorted – although I'd still wear one of their balaclavas when it was freezing, which it always seemed to be. The only sources of heat came from the coal fire and that was only lit when there was enough money for fuel. This meant that we would have to leave the fire until its dying embers were flickering out before we were allowed to chuck more coal on. And if you weren't careful when chucking coal on, the ash would spatter out onto the hearth and you'd get a swipe around your lugs for making a mess.

Fire backed up, mess cleaned up, it was out to play. First stop, pick up my friend Maureen Gee, then off through the tennies (tenements) towards the empty houses.

Maureen Gee was the best of all my best friends. She lived on the first landing in our tenements, directly underneath Mrs Cottier, who was a right pain in the arse. Mrs Cottier was constantly moaning like one of those larger-than-life TV characters you get in *Corrie* or *EastEnders*. Most of her moaning and shouting was because Maureen's mam had a myna bird that used to swear all the time and hardly let up for a break. She used to put the bird outside for some fresh air, placing its cage on the wall within earshot of Mrs Cottier. The myna bird would be effin' and blindin' – 'fuck', 'shite' and 'arsehole' seemed to be its words of choice. Me and Maureen had willingly helped with the bird's vocabulary, and all the swearing would drive Mrs Cottier mad; not that she was some kind of do-gooder, Bible-bashing God-botherer or anything, she just didn't like to hear excessive cursing on her own doorstep.

When my brother Brian got old enough, he was allowed to come with me and Maureen on our adventures. 'Come on, Brian,' I'd shout, and then the two of us would scramble for the front door with our nan's warning ringing in our ears:

'You'd best not slam the door!' Bang! Too late. In our eagerness to get out and play that front door was always slammed.

'Where shall we go today, Brian?' I'd call back to him as he was still fixing his snake belt, while trailing behind. 'Hurry up, dozy!' Then our nan would shout her second warning, this time from the flat window, 'Don't you be going in them bombed houses!' Too late again for her words fell on deaf ears as we disappeared amongst the rubble. Besides, where else was there to play?

Our Brian was so slow to get dressed and yet in every other way he was a live wire. Brian loved sugar butties, and I blame all that bloody sugar for giving him unnatural reserves of energy. One of my earliest recollections was of him standing at the kitchen table almost drooling as Mam sprinkled sugar onto some bread. At the same time he would tap his leg and twitch; also a result of too much sugar. His tapping and twitching drove our mam crackers as she tried to coax him to stop without giving him a complex. But he never stopped, and the more excited he got, the worse his tapping and twitching got. So, as soon as Brian was old enough, I found a way for him to burn off some of his excess energy by introducing him to our incredible adventure playground. The derelict houses waiting to be pulled down numbered in their thousands. These houses were dangerous and therefore, to a kid, the greatest play areas in the world. I remember calling them 'bomdees', which I know sounds like a place in Asia, but I think it meant 'bombed', like in the war. I still don't know if there's a proper spelling for it, but every kid used the word.

Sometimes we were lucky enough to find a length of rope that we could use to make a street swing. Our Brian would put some of his hyper-energy to good use by doing what he did best, climbing. He'd grab the rope, then shinny up the nearest iron lamppost and in no time at all, he would have tied it around one of the lamppost arms. He was definitely the best climber in our gang, like a little monkey. Because he was the one who tied the rope, Brian would always be given the first swing after we'd secured a stick or an old car tyre to the bottom of the rope as a makeshift seat – anything would do as long as our arses could grip it.

The cinemas at that time only ever showed cowboy films, and being from where we were from, we couldn't really relate to them – well, you never saw the Lone Ranger and his horse Silver riding over bricks and rubble, with Tonto shouting, 'Scout say avoid bricks, Kimosabe!' I mean, where we lived was wild, but it looked nothing like the Wild West. So when the cinemas started to show war films like *The Dirty Dozen*, *Where Eagles Dare* and *Von Ryan's Express*, our little gang started playing at war. After all, we did have the perfect backdrop.

Billy, our Brian's mate, was always a bit up himself when it came to playing games. However, he wasn't always that way. A couple of years earlier, Billy was picked on a lot by the kids in his school. 'Does yer mam hide her money under yer soap?' the kids would say, laughing. What they meant was Billy's mam never moved the soap because he was the kid in school who was always dirty and never got a wash. The teacher used to send him out of the classroom to the toilets to wash his face. He would come back with a clean face and a black neck.

A few years later, nobody would mess with Billy because everyone reckoned he was a hard knock. It was an injury he suffered that made us all think he was the toughest lad around. Y'see, Billy and another lad were playing ollies (marbles) in the street, and a few of the ollies rolled off down a grid. He and the lad pulled the grid up so they could get at the ollies, but the grid was so heavy the other lad let go and it came crashing down on Billy's hand. Billy lost two of his fingers that day. Then there was another time I was with Billy, our Brian and two other mates at our favourite derelict house on Upper Duke Street, just down the slope from the Anglican cathedral. We were jumping from a lower roof on to six or more smelly old mattresses, and we must have been jumping from about twenty feet up, but as I said, there was no fear back then and no sign of a Health and Safety Officer. So, as we're risking life and limb, it's Billy's turn to jump. He leaps out and lands on a part only two mattresses thick, a part with a load of bricks underneath. *Snap*! I swear Billy's ankle snapping could be heard from several postcodes away. Then, when I saw his ankle swelling up like a beach ball, I almost vomited.

I remember me and me mates screaming and running up to the main road and heading into the oncoming traffic, waving our arms to try and get someone to stop their car and help us. The first three cars all stopped, thank God, and soon one of them was taking Billy to the hospital, escorted by one of the other cars. I know that might sound strange, a complete stranger carrying your friend off to hospital in their car, but back then, there wasn't the same amount of paranoia or psychos as there are today.

Anyway, that afternoon we had PE in school and when the PE teacher told us to climb up the twenty-foot-high rope to the gym rafters, we told her what had happened to Billy earlier. We shouldn't have bothered, because all she said was that it couldn't happen in her lesson because for one, we were climbing the bleedin' rope and not jumping off it. And two, if we did happen to fall then the gym mat would save us from anything breaking. Gym mat? The mattresses were two-feet thick and Billy still managed to bust his ankle through landing on two of them! But you know at the time her words were reassuring enough to make us climb the rope – back then, we trusted adults a lot more because we didn't have the internet to prove them wrong. Anyway, Billy was in and out of the hospital in no time, and from then on, we were convinced he was super-tough, because if we'd had our fingers chopped off and broken our ankles, we'd have simply died.

Every time we played War, we would all meet up on the holler (a vacant strip of land). Billy was like the boss of the gang and would say, 'I'm gonna be the General!' then pace up and down, just like a general picking his soldiers, as the rest of us were on pins, hoping to be picked first – 'Me, Billy, *me*,' we'd mutter, hoping to get on the winning side, because in the films the Germans never won.

Billy would shout, 'Jimmy, Tommo, Smithy and Brian, you're my soldiers! Paul, Crissy, Maureen, Jonesy and Frank, yous the Germans!' Jonesy didn't like Billy because whenever we split into teams to play soldiers, Billy always insisted that Jonesy be a German. We all got picked to be Germans at one time or another, but Jonesy was always one.

'That's not fair, I don't wanna be a German!' he would shout at Billy, throwing a wobbler. 'I was a German yesterday! Why have I got to be a flippin' German again? The Germans never win, I wanna be an American soldier this time!'

'Well, you can't be,' Billy used to say. 'You're the Jerry because they're from far away and your nan lives in Kirkby and that's far away too. So there, you divvy German!' I can remember the rest of us laughing, but at the same time thinking, that makes sense. Even poor Jonesy thought the same: 'Shurrup!' he would shout, frustrated, sulking and kicking the rubble.

With the two armies sorted, we scattered in opposite directions, making makeshift bunkers amongst the ruined houses. The war wounds we sustained were all real as we scrambled, ran and crawled through the empty, half-knocked-down houses, clambering over bricks, wood and glass without a care in the world. And although we would emerge from the rubble with cuts and grazes, head to toes full of splinters and covered in all kinds of muck, we didn't have a care because it was all in a good day's fun.

I remember the time when Jonesy decided to get back at Billy for making him the designated German for the ten millionth time. The following day, Jonesy planned to get a note to take to Ali's grocery shop to buy some eggs on tick.

'Eggs? What do we need eggs for?' Maureen asked Jonesy.

'Coz when we toss them at each other, we'll know we've been blown up, coz yesterday, when I machine-gunned Tommo, he said I missed him. So I'll get him good and proper with an egg hand grenade, and he can't say it never hit him coz he'll be covered in egg yolk.'

Our mission the next day was going to Ali's for eggs. The four of us trotted into the corner shop and Ali came to the counter. Jonesy stood on tiptoes: 'Ali, my mam said, can she have some eggs?'

'Where's your note?'

'She couldn't find the pen to write a note, Ali, and they're for my dad's dinner.'

'How many eggs does she want? And you'd better not be lying.'

'Nah, I'm not lying, Ali! Honest to God, my mam needs them, I swear.'

Ali handed over six eggs and we left the shop, carefully cradling our precious hand grenades, ready for the battle ahead.

Jonesy made us swear on our mams' lives not to mention anything to Billy about the eggs, so we swore and never mentioned a thing. But it wasn't fair that Jonesy kept three eggs and only gave Maureen and me one egg each. 'That's coz girls can't throw,' he said.

The game started and we lay close to the rubble floor and watched Billy, Brian, Tommo, Smithy and Jimmy holding their Tommy guns – which were made from sticks – searching to find us. But we were on the first floor of the building and so they couldn't see us. All of a sudden, Jonesy stood up and roared, 'CHAAAAARGE!', lobbing the three eggs with all his might, one after the other, straight at the lads. Two eggs missed, but one caught Billy full impact on the side of his head, knocking him flying onto a load of wood with nails sticking out.

Billy lay there motionless for what seemed like forever. We were silent and in shock. Then suddenly, 'You've killed Billy!' Tommo shouted. We ran down to see if Billy was alright, and by the time we got there he was moving and crying. I'll always remember one of the egg yolks was dripping off his face and mixing in with his blood.

'Are you alright, Billy?' Jonesy said, panicked and white as a sheet. Then we all hoisted Billy up and ran him home to his mam. When we got to his mam's flat she was hanging clothes out on the landing. She spotted Billy limping and crying, and immediately took off on him and then us.

'God almighty!' Billy's mam was furious – I think she thought he'd lost more fingers. 'What have I told you about going in them knocked-down houses, hey? And you lot can bugger off before I hit yous all an' don't think I won't be telling your mothers! An' none of yous had best come knocking here for him again – you go on, get down your own end!'

Poor Billy, he got five stitches and a big cogger (bump) on the back of his head that didn't go down for a week. The worst thing was we thought we'd got away with it, until Jonesy's mam went to Ali's to buy some potatoes and he asked her for the egg money. Every one of us got dragged along to Ali's shop. It was like the war was over, we were the war criminals and our mams were MPs, dragging us off for sentencing. We were forced to say sorry to Ali and had to work doing errands and packing potatoes for him until the eggs were paid for. We also got a battering off our dads. I wouldn't look at an egg for ages after that. Things eventually healed over, Billy was out playing with us all again, and because Jonesy felt really bad for landing us all in it, Billy took pity on him and never asked him to be a German ever again.

Our war gang also got into some less heroic goings-on after watching resourceful adults benefiting from the empty properties: removing copper electricity cables and lead gas and water pipes and selling them on to local scrapyards. We saw this as a way to make some easy pocket money and were fortunate to have Packenhams' scrapyard to take what we 'salvaged' off our hands. The people at Pakenhams knew we were little tykes so they were always careful when weighing in our salvage, making sure to check that we hadn't put some heavy, less valuable lead in the copper bag. I like to think that what we were doing was recycling rather than thieving as, from what we witnessed, the demolition contractors made no great effort to recycle – they just seemed intent on flattening the sites with their metal ball and clearing them as quickly as possible. How many square miles of Welsh slate were dumped in a hole somewhere we'll never know. Remember, this was long before home ownership, DIY and recycling, so what hardworking man would want to spend time improving a rundown, rented property?

Going regularly into these empty properties made us

appreciate just how structurally delicate some of them were. The police usually made at least a token effort to chase us out of them and, fearing a cuff across the ear, we fled. I can recall a few incidents where my friends had near-death experiences. In one, a friend jumping from a back-bedroom window was followed to the ground by the large stone windowsill from which he had jumped, and which narrowly missed him by inches. Another time, a friend, being third or fourth to jump from a back-bedroom window on to an apparently sound Yorkshire stone outside toilet roof, went straight through it. Luckily, the roof reached the toilet floor before he did! Apart from scrap metal, those moving out often left unwanted old furniture and other household items, which the scavenging adults and children would take for their own use.

Some years later, I built a small, low-rise lean-to shed in our backyard with materials recycled from the empty houses – I used to house my pet rabbits and mice in it. And I still have a 1930s dictionary salvaged in 1965 from an empty house on Baker Street.

Teenagers also made regular use of the empty houses for what might be termed 'early romantic manoeuvres'. Away from prying adult eyes, the houses were ideal for this throughout the year, keeping them out of the rain and snow during winter. And the darkness didn't seem to matter! These derelict houses also allowed us kids to indulge in acts of wanton vandalism, such as breaking windows, kicking in doors and even knocking down walls at no financial cost to anybody. Happy days!

CHAPTER FOUR

STROKING THE SKY

The first high-rise flats to appear were in Kirkby, on the outskirts of Liverpool. Where once the roads used to be a mile long, now it seemed the buildings were a mile high. At first, and for a lot of people living in the so-called Liverpool slums, there was a sense of jubilation. Apart from the printed posters and pamphlets, most people had never seen a high-rise block, never mind been in one. The pamphlets read like they were going to be relocated to a modern-day utopia, where concrete mega structures stood in aesthetic harmony with green spaces, each supplied with the latest playground equipment for kids and grandkids. Little did they know that these utopian structures would signal the end of their communities. The once-enthusiastic elderly were uprooted from their terraced houses by golden promises that delivered lead-grey tombs. Many of them were moved away from the area, although they had been promised that they would still be around friends and neighbours. Those who stayed to live in the local high-rises, like Entwistle Heights and Milner House, were afraid of the lifts because of the constant power cuts, terrified they might get trapped in one. Instead they became trapped in their flats. No longer able to sit outside their front door chatting to a neighbour on their doorstep, they were left alone with only thoughts of happier times.

After a while even us kids were affected by the changes that were happening. With the communities splitting up, there were hardly any street parties. Trips to Wales, Blackpool and Southport also stopped because there weren't any communities. But kids, in general, are pretty resilient, and where adults saw only the impractical side of high-rises, we regarded them as huge sci-fi-like towers that must have been built just for our amusement.

My family were lucky. When we did end up moving, we weren't forced into a high-rise, we got a nice house all to ourselves with lots of bedrooms and a front and back garden. But we still had all the fun of two looming adventure buildings right on our doorstep. I suppose I would compare it to being a grandparent – you can have all the good times with your grandkids, but you get to give them back at the end of the day. We could play in the high-rises with the friends who lived there, then return to the comfort of our houses.

Jenny was one of the kids that I hung around with at the age of twelve. She lived in Entwistle Heights on the eighteenth or nineteenth floor. Whatever floor it was, you could see right across Liverpool, all the way to Wales. Entwistle was built in 1965 and was twenty-two floors high. It was built to house around 1,000 people in its 168-flat, 4-acre plot. I remember when it was first finished and there was a big celebration as the first tenants moved in. The concrete walls looked immaculate and almost gleaming back then. A few years later, however, and the utopian mega-structure resembled an old block in East Berlin. The concrete had dulled, worn and discoloured. Graffiti spread from one end of a wall to the other. Glass was smashed everywhere and stuck in the soles of your shoes as you walked, making your shoes sound like you were tap dancing. The playground equipment was rusted and twisted, and green spaces now overgrown weed plots strewn with dog doo.

On a brighter note, we loved the high-rises. From Jenny's flat, overlooking Liverpool, you felt like you were floating on a cloud. You were so close to the sky, you could poke it with your finger. The only time I had ever been that high up was when my mam took me and our Brian to the top of the Anglican cathedral tower and we were kicked out because me and Brian were spitting off the tower to see if we could hit a passer-by on the head.

The ride in the steel lifts in Entwistle Heights and its sister block, Milner House, was so exciting to a kid who – apart from the lifts in Lewis's and a few other department stores – had never been allowed in a lift unaccompanied by an adult. We would slam our hands against the lift buttons, making sure the button to every floor lit up. And whenever an adult got in the lift, they would glare at us as the floor arrival bell sounded, followed by the door opening on every floor. At first the lifts ran perfectly well and they were kept clean, but a few years down the line, they were constantly breaking down and always smelled of pee. In fact, the lifts smelled so badly, it made you wonder just what those lift-pissers were drinking to make their pee smell so rank!

Boys liked hanging around the high-rises, and often there were boys living there who had been moved in from other broken communities across Liverpool. These boys were exciting because they could act hard, like real bad guys, as nobody knew their backgrounds or if they were really tough at all. They would sit in the thoroughfare between the Entwistle and Milner blocks. This space was shadowy and added to their air of mystery. The toughest boy, and therefore the gang leader, was a kid called Leon. He was a matted-haired, huge kid, who claimed his family were gypsies who'd become so pissed off with travelling in a caravan, they'd put in for a council flat. Leon told us that his uncle was crazy-mental, that he came from some strange country I could never remember, and had killed three men who attacked him when he lived in this strange country I couldn't remember (I think he said it was in Europe). Apparently, these guys tried mugging his uncle because he'd been given gold by the king.

Leon was the worst storyteller ever – totally crap – but no one had the bottle to tell him in case he got his crazy-mental uncle to kill us the same way he killed the three men who tried mugging him. According to Leon, his uncle was so padded out with the gold he'd got off the king of 'wherever', he dived into a local lake with the three men in pursuit. He held onto the men as the gold pulled him and them to the bottom of the lake, and he kept holding on until they drowned, but he survived because he was a champion swimmer and a world record holder at holding his breath. He then swam up and out of the lake, leaving the gold, which he retrieved at a later date. But he was then spotted by police as he was retrieving the gold, with the three bodies floating around him, so he and his family were forced to go on the run in their Romany caravan. It turned out Leon was as full of shit as he was a crap storyteller. In truth, he'd moved into the area, having lived in a tenement in Runcorn for most of his life. He and his boys always smoked cigarettes and sometimes had bottles of beer they would share with us.

'Do you want a swig, Crissy?' one boy would ask, holding a bottle out to me.

'Only if you haven't spat in it.'

My mam didn't like me hanging around with Jenny. Not that she didn't like her or anything, it was just because she lived in the 'heights' as we called them. Mam wasn't soft, she knew we were hanging around Jenny a lot more once we discovered Leon and his friends lived in the same block as her. And although she never smelt ciggies or alcohol on our breath, she knew we were up to some kind of no good. I never got to kiss any of those lads that hung around the heights, but it didn't really matter because I flirted with them and I had a good imagination. Each night, I'd get home and think about the one lad called Rodney – I could see myself laughing with him, telling jokes, and him being very impressed. Then I would imagine him calling for me, with me answering the door all done up to the nines in one of my Aunty Sandra's lovely frocks. His jaw drops as he goes all googly-eyed. We spend an amazing day together and – just before my mam calls me in – we share a perfect kiss. A perfect kiss only happens in your imagination. A real kiss is never perfect, as you might drool into their mouth or have a runny nose that ends up mingling into the kiss; they might have eaten garlic, or even worse, they could end up transferring bits of their last meal into your mouth. Ah, Rodney, he may have been the runt of the high-rise boys, but he was also my first love, although he didn't know it!

Whereas I aimed low and dreamt about the boy in the gang who was a runt and a nerd, Jenny set her sights on the prize, the 'on-the-run Runcorn gypsy' himself, Leon. Their romance lasted all of two nights and both times she was FAFO'd (fondled and fucked off).

My fondest memories of these high-rises – besides seeing Rodney, of course – were of the windiest days of the year. Because the towers were at the top of Parliament Street, at the city's highest point, the wind used to blow from off the River Mersey all the way up Parliament Street and would hit the tower blocks full force. On those windy days we could stand between the buildings, open our coats and hold them out to catch the wind, which would lift us into the air and fly us through the thoroughfare. Sometimes we would take off and get slammed into a wall and roll along it, ending up spread-eagled on the ground. On windy days, the boys would deliberately wear longer coats so they could be lifted even higher into the air. I suppose it was dangerous, but as I've said before, back then the words 'health' and 'safety' were never used in the same sentence.

Entwistle Heights and Milner House were demolished in 1986, along with lots of other high-rises that were deemed 'eyesores'. And once again families were dispersed across the city.

CHAPTER FIVE

SPRING HEELS
AND PYRAMIDS

For some reason, Liverpool has always had more than its fair share of ghost stories, monsters and even wild-eyed eccentrics. Nowadays, kids have the naughty Elf on the Shelf to keep them in check, but in the 1960s we had Spring-Heeled Jack. Now, Spring-Heeled Jack was just one of the many monsters and scary stories that terrified us so badly, me and my friends were too scared to go out after dark. This was mostly when I was a kid in the sixties and seventies, but I can remember more recent times when I would be walking along in the dark and suddenly remember one of those scary tales. I'd be twisting my neck one way and then the other, while threatening to hit whatever was in the shadows with a tray of doner kebab meat doused in garlic sauce!

I blame my mam for most of these nervous moments as it was her duty to scare the shite out of us kids whenever she told us stories. There was George the ghost on the fifth floor of the Adelphi Hotel. Then the poltergeist at 44 Penny Lane – admittedly, Mam hadn't heard the word 'poltergeist', so she just called it a crazy or mischievous ghost. There was the Black Phantom of the Empire Theatre, and then there was Speke Hall's ghostly mother. Speke Hall was a stately home that we used to go to on school visits under the guise of educating us in the history of Liverpool. In truth, I think the school decided on visiting there because they didn't know what to do with us and they didn't have the funds to take us elsewhere. Whatever their reasons, us kids were happy to play along as we found Speke Hall fascinating as it was rumoured to be haunted. Over the years, visitors had heard a lady screaming and crying in the corridors. The story goes that this lady had thrown her baby out of a window, centuries before, for some strange reason. So, whenever we visited, we used to be on the lookout for a floating baby ghost and the ghost of its mam, who really shouldn't have thrown the baby out in the first place if she was gonna go on whingeing about it for the next few centuries, the daft cow! However, no matter how many times we shushed each other as we traversed the Speke Hall corridors, we never once got to hear the screaming lady.

On a level of one to ten, with ten being the scariest, most of my mam's scary stories rated a four, maybe – at a push – a five. Her scariest rated a six and even a seven. Those sixes and sevens would make you keep the light on all night and could give you extreme nightmares.

'Mam, don't put the light out!'

'Oh, Crissy, you're too old for needing the light on!'

'No I'm not, leave it on!'

'Do you want me to tell your friends you sleep with the light on?'

'Okay, turn it off.'

I would always be caught out by the 'Tell your friends' threat and cave in – except, that is, when the scare level rated a ten. The only one of my mam's stories that got a ten for scariness was the one about Spring-Heeled Jack.

'Do you want me to tell your friends you sleep with the light on?'

'Tell who you like, it's staying on!'

Spring-Heeled Jack was a legend to some and a real horror to others, and I can still remember the very first time Mam told us the tale of the tall, skinny man with long, clawed fingers, who leapt from roof to roof, searching for children. But unlike other old legends and stories where you might have a creature that only seeks out the naughty children or those kids who refuse to eat their greens, Spring-Heeled Jack just searched for children, full stop. He didn't care if you were naughty or nice, he wasn't Santa Claus, he just wanted kids so he could take them away and most probably eat them. Mam hadn't even mentioned that he ate children, me and my twisted imagination added that bit just to terrify myself even more. From the moment she told me that story the seal was broken, the cat was out of the bag, Pandora's Box wide open for business. I remember it slowly dawning on her what a mistake she'd made in telling us that story. My parents' heads must have been wrecked because every time we stepped out to go and visit a relative, or we were on our way back from having visited one, me and our Brian would fight over who got to walk closest to Dad.

'I'm walking with my dad, you walk with Mam!' I'd shout, but Brian would nestle right into Dad because he was smaller and could fit into his leg space. Mam knew that we weren't choosing him over her, it was just that Dad was bigger and would probably have a better chance of fighting off Spring-Heeled Jack without fainting. He used to shake his head, look at Mam and say, 'You see what your stories have done, Margie. I can hardly walk for these two!' Mam would tell us to stop being silly.

'But Spring-Heeled Jack's gonna get us!' Brian said.

'And eat us!' I added.

'If you think he's jumping on the roof, keep your eyes on the pavement,' said Mam, hoping this would make us feel better because she'd told us that Spring-Heeled Jack couldn't get you unless you looked straight at him. However, our mam telling us the best ways to avoid being grabbed by Jack just solidified our belief that he existed. There was even one Christmas when my dad, a little merry after having a quick after-work drink with the lads, mentioned to me and Brian that there was a rumour going round that Spring-Heeled Jack had kidnapped Father Christmas and stolen his clothes so he could come down all the chimneys and take the kids.

'Eddie, what the hell would you tell them that for?' Mam took off. 'It's alright for you, coz it's not gonna be you they're crying at, come bedtime!'

Dad looked a little guilty, but you could tell he wanted to laugh.

We – me and Brian – did not look forward to Christmas Eve night that year. And neither did most of me mates, because I told them all what my dad had said. Well, why should we be shitting ourselves and our mates not having a care in the world? You're supposed to share adversity. I mean, isn't that what friends are for? Anyhow, to this day, I'm still freaked by the idea of Spring-Heeled Jack, only now in my head, I see him as a stringy long creature dressed in a mourning suit, or even a stringy long creature wearing a Santa outfit – thanks for that, Dad.

But, like I mentioned, the wild-eyed eccentrics of Liverpool could be just as scary as any legendary monsters. I remember spending one Halloween sitting next to one of the largest bonfires I have ever seen. It was on a wasteland off Harrowby Street, a street that crossed Granby Street. Even though it was only Halloween, some idiot kid had set fire to the bonfire to scare his mate, who was hiding amongst the timber and debris that made up the stack. The kid's mate climbed out in time not to get burnt, but the fire raged to a point where nobody could put it out, so everyone sat around watching the bonfire a few days in advance of Bommie (Bonfire) Night. I had got a potato off a friend who lived off Granby and we were now listening to stories being told by three hippy-like elderly women. As usual in storytelling, when the sky grows darker, the stories grow darker too. The first woman told a story about a Jamaican man who was about to marry a woman he had pulled from the sea – no, she wasn't a flippin' mermaid – and he fell in love and asked her to marry him three days after saving her. She said yeah, and everything was all going well. The priest was about to start his speech when the groom looked down and saw that the woman had hooves, cloven hooves like the Devil. Yeah, that's what we thought, crap story or what?

That story got the first hippy booed off. The next woman's story was as bad as the first and equally disturbing because she kept mentioning how naked the woman was in the story. The third old hippy woman's story was really creepy. Now, I have heard this story since and it tends to change in detail, but I'll tell it to you the way me and my Indian friend Marjebene heard it – no, not Margarine! The old hippy woman said that there was a graveyard attached to St Andrew's church on Rodney Street that has a tall pyramid tomb standing amongst the gravestones. And that the tomb belonged to a man called Billy Mackenzie. Billy was a zillionaire or something, filthy rich, and he loved to gamble. One day, Billy's bored because he can't find anyone who's good enough to play him at cards, so he challenges the Devil. Mid-story, I suddenly pipe up, 'Where did he meet the Devil?' and I'm immediately shushed by everyone, including Marjebene. The old hippy woman continued, describing what the Devil looked like when he turned up and what kind of cards he was holding in his claws. I shout out, 'The Devil's got hooves, not claws!' and the old hippy says, 'Only on his back legs, girl!' She continues by saying that this Billy bet the Devil his soul because he was sure that he was the best card player in Liverpool. But Billy lost his soul with one turn of the cards. The Devil said he would collect Billy's soul on the day he died, the moment he was buried. So, Billy makes sure he's never buried and leaves his brother instructions as to what to do when he dies.

Soon after Billy died and his brother had the pyramid built and put Billy in it. However, instead of putting Billy in a coffin, like you do, he followed Billy's written wishes and sat his corpse up at the head of a gambling table, a glass of wine in one hand and a winning hand of cards in the other. This was so that the Devil couldn't tell if Billy was dead or alive and therefore couldn't collect his soul.

Me and Marjebene were disturbed by this story, and by the way the hippy woman was cackling like an old witch throughout. Then, just as I realised my potato had turned to charcoal, the hippy woman added, 'The Devil still searches through the streets of Liverpool every night at around…' she glanced at her watch, '…this time, looking for a soul to replace Billy's, a soul he can drag back down to Hell with him!'

Nobody would walk me home that night, and I had to make the journey on my own. I twisted and turned, and even walked backwards with every noise or whistle of the wind, all the time cursing Marjebene for not even asking her dad to walk me part way – flippin' cow! Needless to say, she wasn't on my top ten list of 'friends to hang around with' from then on.

CHAPTER SIX

THE ROYAL FAMILY

Now, let me first point out that the following isn't a chapter about that well-loved BBC sitcom *The Royle Family*, starring my old mucker and fellow Scouser Ricky Tomlinson. This chapter is about exactly what it sounds like: the British royal family, or at least one or two of them. Okay, I can hear your brains working overtime, wondering why in heaven's name would I put this subject in a book about me growing up in Liverpool. Well, to paraphrase Will Shakespeare, 'There's method in the madness.' I can think of three clear memories in the sixties and seventies where the royal family, or a member of them, featured in my life. The first was Prince Charles.

A while after my nan died, we moved into our house in Chatsworth Street – it must have been in 1969 or thereabouts. I remember Prince Charles had recently become Prince of Wales and at the time there was a large picture of Charlie featured in the *Liverpool Echo* newspaper. My dad had bought the *Echo*, read it and left it on his chair. I looked through it, searching for the comic strips, and came across the picture of Prince Charles. He was only young and looked dead smart and all prince-like. It was the first time I felt a connection with any of the royal family; I suppose it was because he was now the Prince of Wales, and Wales was one of my favourite places to go on holiday – although Colomendy, not so much.

That photograph of Charlie rekindled something in my mind that I hadn't thought since being a wee nipper, that real-life princes could be the same as the ones you read about in fairy tales, the ones who did heroic and noble deeds like jousting and rescuing damsels in distress. I thought it would be nice to have a real Prince Charming on my bedroom wall, so I swiped my dad's paper and cut it out. Cutting through the paper, I held the scissors more carefully than anything I'd done; I didn't even breathe in case I went wrong, holding my breath all the time like an army sniper. Once I'd cut the picture out, I placed it carefully on the bed. I was going to put my dad's paper back on the chair, but I knew if he spotted that I'd been chopping up his paper he'd have given me a slap, whereas if I hid it, he'd think he'd mislaid it in the pub or somewhere. So I stashed the paper under the mattress then went off to find some flour. Nowadays, you would use PVA glue, back then it was a mix of flour and water you used as glue, and it really did do the same job. So I pasted the flour-glue all over the back of the picture and stuck it to my bedroom wall.

I loved that picture a lot more than I loved Prince Charles

because of the effort that went into hanging it, and because it reminded me that I was growing up, having a picture of a man on my bedroom wall. Then we had to move to a new house and I realised short of chiselling the picture out of the plaster, I was going to have to leave it behind. That damn flour-and-water concoction had gone above and beyond and stuck my prince to the bedroom wall for ever. I was devastated to be leaving that picture behind, and when I told my mam and dad, they were really understanding, although I'm sure I heard them having a little giggle as I left the room. After that, I didn't really follow anything the royal family did for a long time.

Then along came my second run-in with the royals and definitely one to remember: The Sex Pistols singing 'God Save the Queen'. What a messed-up song and we all flamin' loved it. The Sex Pistols released the song in May 1977 and the whole nation was to celebrate the queen's Silver Jubilee in June of that year with street parties right across Britain. The whole nation was divided as to whether or not they should listen to something so anti-monarchy. But all the teenagers, myself included, listened to it whenever we got a chance; whenever my husband at the time wasn't lurking around. I even had a T-shirt with the song lyrics 'No Future' written across it that I'd made myself.

I remember at the time a lot of people thought the song was an attack on the royal family and also an attack on the British government, who, in the lyrics, are referred to as 'The fascist regime/They made you a moron/A potential H bomb'.

I didn't know what a 'regime' was, but I must have looked like a fuckin' moron, having left the letter 'e' off the word 'future'!

The third royal run-in was the queen's Silver Jubilee on 7 June 1977. To have an occasion where HM the queen was coming to our city called for more than a half of ale and a tiny flag waving. Nah, Liverpool brought out the big guns of national pride. There were street parties on every street. Long tables and short were lined together and filled with cakes and lots of other food and fizzy drinks and alcohol. The puff pastry manufacturers must have been hard-pressed to keep up with demand because every street party consumed at least a thousand sausage rolls over the course of a day. The whole event was an excuse for me and my friend Jules to wear our punkish gear inspired by The Sex Pistols' record release a couple of weeks before. We thought we were so radical and cool, dressed in our not-too-punk jackets with a few safety pins, as we headed down Upper Duke Street to catch a glimpse of the Queen and Phil as they went past.

I'd left my little one with a friend for the night as her father couldn't be trusted to look after himself, never mind a two-year-old. I really needed to get away from what was happening in my life at that time and the Jubilee was the ideal excuse. Of course, I never let him know where I was really off to, not that he would have given a rat's arse. Anyway, Jules and I stood opposite the Liverpool Institute School for Boys, where Paul McCartney had once attended and which is now his performing arts college. The railings of the school were smothered by rowdy schoolboys dressed in black blazers with their green emblems and ties. I remember four of the boys pointing at us and one started shouting to us, 'Hey, have you just fell outta bed?' He was referring to our spiky hair. I started laughing because Jules's hair was way more spiky than mine because she'd had hers professionally styled that way. My spiky hair was due to a handful of American hair gel so I could wash it out later before going home to him.

Jules didn't think the boy's comment was funny because she was pure punk. She ran over to the lad, without saying a word, and kicked him in the shin. The boy laughed at her and jeered, 'Is that how spiky twats kick?', forcing a laugh, but we knew he wanted to cry his eyes out because Jules was wearing steel toe-capped Doc Martens. As the lad hobbled away with his mates, we suddenly heard cheering in the distance. The cheering got closer and closer until we spotted her, standing up in the back of an open-top Rolls-Royce. Everyone was cheering and shouting, 'Congratulations, Your Majesty,' and other greetings. She was dressed in a pink coat and hat and she looked lovely.

I couldn't believe that the Queen of England was right there in front of me on a Liverpool street on the border of Liverpool 8, Toxteth. Besides Jesus Christ, The Beatles and The Jackson 5, I had never heard of anyone as famous as Queen Liz. I remember there was a group of girls in yellow leotards performing a rehearsed dance in the road, and the queen looked and smiled at them and they were so happy and proud. And it was at that point I started feeling a little bit of shame. I'd come along to see the queen doing the whole punk thing, trying to make a statement, and there were these kids who'd probably rehearsed their dance routine every day for weeks and were now happy as Larry to catch a single royal nod and smile. I immediately fastened my jacket so you couldn't see my 'No Futur' misspelled T-shirt and joined in with the waving.

After Queen Liz passed by and the crowds moved on, me and Jules hit the street parties, going from one party to another, mine-sweeping alcohol and cadging any free booze and cigs we could get our paws on. 'Hiya, lad. Giz a ciggy,' Jules would say to the young fellas who were pissed. Not once did she get a refusal. In fact, we came away with pocketfuls of ciggies from lads who were trying to impress while having a bit of a flirt with us. When we were fully tanked, me and Jules headed off, almost falling into the city centre to get extra shit-faced.

After that, and to this day, I've never really had any reason to like or dislike the royals or what they're about. To be honest, the subject never came up in the circles I hung around in. I will say this, though: when Lady Di came along, I always thought she was a genuinely lovely soul and I and everyone I knew were heartbroken when she died...poor chick.

CHAPTER SEVEN

FROM YOUTH CLUBS TO NIGHT CLUBS

L iverpool in the seventies, like cities all over the country, had youth clubs dotted about everywhere. In fact, there were so many youth clubs, if you didn't want to go to a club where you knew there was a bully, or where someone was after you – because, as a kid, you always seemed to be saying someone's after you – or if you didn't want to go to a club where everyone knew you once peed your pants because you couldn't make it to the toilet in time, then there were lots and lots of options.

The youth clubs I used to hang around were The Rodney (Rods), The Penny Wreck, The Unity Girls Club, which had a youth club adjacent to it called – yeah, you guessed it – The Unity Boys Club, The Methodist Centre (Meth), The Caribbean Centre and The David (Davy) Lewis. The Rods, or Rodney Youth Centre as it was officially known, was the old Ritz Roller Rink on the corner off Catherine and Myrtle

Streets. It was a big old building that me and the mates who didn't mind getting bloodied knees and sore ankles used to frequent on certain nights of the week. I remember you could buy a box of broken biscuits as you went in and that was brilliant because they sometimes put chocolate bars and sweets inside.

Rods was pure mayhem; lots of kids of all ages screaming at the tops of their voices, skating at top speed on roller skates that were falling to bits. 'One size fits all,' the man behind the skate counter would say as he adjusted a tiny skate that might fit the foot of a three-year-old to fit a size eleven adult foot. Once you put the skates on and adjusted the flimsy strap that held it to your foot, you were off like a shot straight across the parquet flooring of the skating rink. More often than not you would accidentally crash into the person coming the other way. Other times you would try to take them out on purpose, especially if it was someone from a rival tenement. Sometimes you would deliberately crash into a guy if you thought he was nice-looking – although once you did, he might give you a kick or even rag the fuck out of your hair as we were only kids, remember.

Me and my group of mates always liked to play like the older lads who took skating to the next level by doing the 'skate jump'. The skate jump involved rounding up lots of nerdy kids and forcing them to lie down in the centre of the rink, side by side, then one of the tougher lads – or bullies – would skate at breakneck speed and try to jump over the nerdy lads. Now and then, the leap was successful, but for the most part, two or three nerdy lads would end up with skate track marks on their chests or faces. Another favourite with the older lads was chasing each other around the upstairs balcony that circled the rink where, if cornered, you would quickly climb over the balcony rail and jump, landing with a crash on the parquet below. The crashing noise was usually our roller skates exploding on impact, the wheels flying off in all directions. 'Out!' the man would shout when he spotted us laughing our heads off, while limping around on wheel-less, twisted roller skates, 'And don't bother coming in for a week!'

We didn't mind getting barred for a week or even longer as all of the other youth clubs we went to had discos, and all the fittest, older boys went to the youth discos. The Meth had a disco on a Thursday, with a DJ called Ivan – who had a gap in his teeth and was nicknamed 'The Russian' – who went on to DJ nearly all of the youth discos in and around Liverpool 8. This was great because I liked the music he played, which was mostly imported Disco and RnB from the States. I suppose the disco I attended the most was the Penny Wreck, only because my friends were lazy pains in the arse and most times refused to walk to the other, much better discos that were further away. One of our school teachers, Mr Newby, ran the Penny Wreck. The reason it was given that name was that it cost a penny to get in. It had a tuck shop and table tennis like the other clubs and football for the lads.

Me and me mate Maureen Gee used to sit and watch the lads playing football and showing off, doing tricks and keepy-uppys. They liked us watching them because lads like showing off to girls, even when they don't fancy them. We'd be smiling at them, cheering them on, flirting and whispering. Maureen would say, 'Would you kiss him?' and I'd be like, 'Have you seen the flamin' gob on him? You could use those teeth for goal posts!' She always laughed at my comments and that encouraged me to get more creative with them: 'And have you seen his snotty nose? He's got more green hanging than the bleedin' footy pitch!' We'd keep commenting, laughing, and taking the piss out of the lads, until we spotted one we liked. You could always tell the ones we thought were nice-looking because the moment we mentioned their name we'd start giggling, not laughing, and hitting each other on the arm. But apart from a slow dance at the end of the discos – on those rare occasions when a lad bothered to ask you up – we never saw any action in those youth clubs.

At the time of going to discos and hanging out with lads – even if they were only kicking a football at us – me and the girls were becoming a lot more conscious of how we looked. Make-up wasn't freely given by your relatives back then and it was like some kind of commodity, almost like gold or something. If you did have an older sister or an aunty who you asked if you could borrow some of their make-up, they wouldn't even grace you with an answer, they would just laugh and walk away, and you certainly couldn't afford to buy any make-up of your own. I could imagine walking into Lewis's make-up department – the doors of which were right under Dickie Lewis's dickie – and clambering up to the counter to ask one of the women, 'What mascara have you got, girl?'

and seeing her look back at me with a bemused look through the twenty layers of shovelled-on make-up the Lewis's beauty staff wore on their faces. So, with no hope of buying make-up, you would have to try biting your lips to make them look redder and pinching your cheeks to make them appear rosier. Hair was a problem too, because nearly all me mates had Afro hair that they wanted to relax and straighten because it was so hard to comb through. I was the exact opposite and would have given anything to have lovely curly hair; unfortunately, I didn't have that much to curl.

The American base was in Burtonwood, so Jackie used to get the bus there to buy the Afro Sheen off the Yanks on the base, which she would use to relax her hair. If she couldn't be arsed going to Burtonwood, then she would drag me along to Abercromby Street, off Upper Parliament Street, where there was a club – All Nations – where the Yanks used to go to get drunk and stoned. Me and Jackie would hang around at the side of the club to see if any of the Yanks had brought Afro Sheen with them. I think Jackie thought they'd just say, 'Oh yeah, ma'm,' and squeeze a load of Afro Sheen on her head. It never happened, but we still used to hang around, saying to the Yanks, 'Hey, mister, can we mind your car?' and most of them would give us money. We took our jobs seriously and would march up and down, keeping a lookout for anyone trying to nick the cars or steal the emblems off the front of them – a favourite thing for kids to do back then. The Yanks would sometimes give us a shilling for minding their cars, other times they would be too pissed to remember us so we'd get sod all.

My mam used to say, 'Don't yous be hanging round that Yank club like little brazzers!' We didn't even know what 'brazzers' were. Then we found out that they were the women we'd been jealous of that used to go in the Yank club dressed to the nines, with nice make-up and immaculate hair. As well as hanging around the All Nations Club, me and Maureen also hung around the shebeens that popped up here and there in Liverpool 8. Shebeens masqueraded as nightclubs, but they were really houses where they played lots of loud music and had Jamaican and West Indian food, like black-eyed peas and rice. The shebeen would sell all kinds of alcohol without a licence and so would only be open for a couple of days before getting raided by the police. God only knows what me and Maureen must have looked like, dancing around outside the shebeens, but you just couldn't help dancing to all the different music they played. Sometimes it would be Ska and reggae, other times, American soul and Motown. Those places were my first introduction to seeing what nightclubs were like, and what went on in them.

As we got older, we tired of the youth club discos and hanging around the shebeens and American clubs. We could now afford make-up and so we headed for the city centre clubs. The Sink was a whole different ball game to the club on Upper Parliament Street. It was a club located on Hardman Street, opposite the famous Blind School, and was in the basement of the Rumblin' Tum Bar, now the location of one of Liverpool's most famous clubs – The Magnet. The Sink played soul music and it was one of the first proper clubs that me and my friends could get in. I remember as you walked in, the door staff would give you a numbered sink-plug on a chain, which meant you'd paid.

Myself and Maureen were too young to get in legally, in fact we must have been twelve or thirteen, God help us, so we had to make ourselves look a lot older than we were. Platform shoes gave me an extra four inches of height. I had on one of my Aunty Sandra's maxi-frocks, and I stuffed my bra with white socks so I looked like I had boobs. I remember our Sandra would see me trying to sneak out of the house wearing some of her clothes and shout something like, 'That had better not be my underskirt!' And she'd start ragging it off me. But I'd usually leg it before she sussed me.

Sandra was stunning, she and her cousin, Annette Paige. The two of them looked like supermodels. Me and me mates were all in awe and slightly jealous of them. My friends used to say, 'What the hell happened to you, Crissy?' And I used to agree with the cheeky sods an' all. Sandra had beautiful teeth and she never swore. She loved The Monkees and had a tape machine that we'd borrow and listen to the tunes she'd recorded. She would always catch us playing them and batter us, but she was a lovely person and someone I wished I was a lot more like at the time, hence the reason I borrowed all her stuff.

The doormen on The Sink were easy-going and let me in even though I was all over the place, trying to balance in my massive platform shoes. I swear to God they were so tall, I used to get friggin' vertigo whenever I wore them! Inside, the club was like any other basement club – dark, but with coloured lights flashing here and there to give you a peek at who you might recognise on the dance floor.

Everyone who went to The Sink could dance. I think it was because most of the men and women had been going out to proper clubs for years and had picked it up watching the American sailors do their thing. Me and me mates thought we were okay dancers till we went there, although, to be fair, we were hindered by having to dance in sky-high heels. The first night we went to The Sink, me and every one of me mates got chatted up loads, and I remember thinking how amazing it was because we were having a real drink that was bought for us by some good-looking guys.

After a couple of jars, me and my friend Janet decided we'd take to the dance floor and proceeded to stagger over, near some other girls who were dancing to Marvin Gaye's 'Too Busy Thinking About My Baby'. Suddenly, Janet starts pissing herself laughing. I started laughing too, as you do, even though I didn't have the slightest clue as to what she was laughing at. But we were tipsy, so that was good enough for me. Then I noticed that the women next to us were staring at me; half the club was staring at me too. I was in my element, thinking they must be staring because I was such a good dancer. I must have looked like a right dickhead, shaking my arse and thinking I'm all that, then I noticed the two women were laughing along with Janet. She finally managed to spit out, between her guffawing, just two words: 'Yer boobs!' I looked down and there they were, glowing like something out of a fifties B-movie. Y'see, The Sink's dance floor had a very large blacklight, or ultra-violet lamp, as we called them back then. And this light was right over my head and had made the whites of the socks I'd stuffed in my bra shine like fog lamps.

'Oh, hell!' I shouted as I legged it off the dance floor. 'I'm getting off, I look like a right knob now!'

But Janet, good enough, stopped laughing and told me to go and fix them in the loo. So, there's me, trying to cover me glowing orbs as I head straight into the ladies'. Once in, I pulled the socks out, lobbed them down the loo and then rejoined Janet at the bar. I remember as we left the club in the early hours, two of the doormen staring at me and frowning like something was missing. They probably went looking in the Lost and Found – 'Whose tits are these? They're a bit woolly!'

We always liked The Sink Club, and even when we started getting into other clubs, we still used to go back to The Sink when we wanted a nice atmosphere where you could chill and listen to great music. They also used to have live bands on certain nights of the week. Some of the bands were famous and had frontmen like Roy Ayers and Gregory Isaacs. Other singers that performed there weren't famous at the time, but went on to become world-famous – singers like Freddie Mercury and Brian May when they still played with their old band, Smile.

Liverpool had its fair share of great nightclubs, and quite a few of them would let us in. There was the Babalou, where anyone of any age could get in and that's why it was nicknamed the 'Baby-lou'. Almost every night the Babalou was raided by police for underage drinking. You'd be dancing away to a great song and then you'd hear the DJ 'George Spence' shout over the mic, 'Everyone out, it's the pigs!' and two doormen would open the back doors so everyone could escape before the police came piling in. I have to admit, there was something funny going on there because in all the times the Babalou got raided, I never once spotted any police. I reckon it was just a con so they could shut the club early once people had paid and started to slow down their alcohol consumption towards the end of the night.

The Time Piece (the TP) was a cool club that stood a street away from the Babalou. It never got raided so if you were allowed in by the very large, Afro'd Mr Sunsher (the head doorman), you were in for a brilliant night of RnB and lots of flirting with some of L8's sexiest black and mixed-race fellas. My other favourite club – where they weren't too fussy about your age – was the Beachcomber (the Beachy). It was in the same vicinity as the Babalou and the TP, but this club played all kinds of music, and so had a mix of white, black, Chinese and every other race and colour. The first time that me, Maureen and Jane went to the Beachy – Jane didn't get on with Janet, so you would only get one of them coming out at a time – we were shocked. 'Eeeeeh!' said Jane, 'they've got a dirty stripper on!' And they did have an'all; halfway through the night, the music suddenly changed to something sleazy as hell. Then out pops the stripper – who looked about fifty, wearing kinky underwear and a school teacher's gown and board – and she starts writhing round in front of a load of horny lads while sucking a lollipop, the dirty mare!

Now, I'd never seen anything like it in my life before, and I was stunned that someone could not give two fucks, lashing her kit off in front of a whole club full of men and women. I never went back to the Beachy for ages after that, although the stripper wasn't the only reason. Jane had got the doorman – who was her best friend's fella – to let us in that night, as it was a members-only club, but when I said I was gonna go to the Beachy with Janet – who Jane hated – Jane got the doorman to say we couldn't come in. We weren't that arsed anyway as there were plenty of clubs to go to, including the Nightsbridge, Top Rank, the She and, of course, the Cavern Club.

One thing that springs to mind when mentioning the Cavern Club is the cloakroom attendant who later became Cilla Black. Now, Cilla wasn't one of my fave singers, but that's probably because when she hit it big in 1964, I was only listening to The Beatles. But years later, when I was going to nightclubs, I started listening to her songs because my friend Carla always played them in her room when we were getting ready to go out for the night.

Carla worked as a cloakroom attendant the same way Cilla had years before. She looked a bit like Cilla, but she couldn't sing and she worked in the Grafton Rooms, not the Cavern Club. The Grafton Rooms had been a popular dance club as far back as World War Two and was once the place to go if you wanted to boogie with American GIs and the British soldiers. In the late sixties and seventies, the Grafton earned the nickname 'The Grab-a-Granny Club'. I'm sure a lot of you reading this will remember the Monday Grab-a-Granny night. All the young guys used to pile down the club, looking for the more mature ladies who – they thought – might be more worldly and less hard-to-get than the more cautious, less experienced girls in other clubs. Most of the women in the Grafton at that time had the same stand-off attitude as any sensible girl when it came to one-night stands, but there were exceptions. There were those who fancied younger guys, others were out to get back at cheating or abusive husbands, some were drunk, and others were randy little hussies out for a bonk off a handsome young lad. For the most part, these ladies were out for a bit of fun and a harmless snog. Mention the Grafton to an old Liverpool taxi driver and he'll most likely tell you that was the place where he met his wife.

By the age of seventeen I had my own council flat at 101 Smithdown Lane and so I could stay out all night if I wanted without my mam or Dad worrying themselves to death. It was far easier to get a flat back then because there were hardly any checks; if you wanted somewhere, then you could apply one week and have a flat the next. At that time Susan Leigh (a girl I had hung around with in school until her parents moved to Widnes) was the main friend of choice to frequent the nightclubs with. I had other mates who came along but, unlike Susan, they weren't reliable. She was reliable because she was a bit of a pisshead and would be dressed in her heels and best frock before you could finish suggesting going out for a piss-up and a dance. Unlike nowadays, the clubs back then all closed at 2 a.m. Shock, horror! I hear those young'uns amongst you gasp. Yes, two o'clock was the time the city closed, with the exception of those clubs and bars that were slipping backhand donations to the police fund, and those places would never let us stay behind as we weren't really mixing in the right circles. So, as soon as the lights came on at the end of the night, and after having your arse groped for the final fifteen minutes by some half-pissed lad who almost fell asleep on your shoulder, you grabbed your coat from the cloakroom, ran outside and hailed a black cab up to Liverpool 8.

Toxteth had some of the most well-known nightclubs in Liverpool that had been in business as far back as the war. Most of the clubs were named after African countries and were owned and run by African men who knew how to deal with the seriously dodgy punters. People came from all over Liverpool to go to the clubs that ran the length and breadth of Upper Parliament Street and Princes Avenue. Back in the fifties and sixties, those clubs were the first stop if you were looking for somewhere with lots of atmosphere, or if you were a sailor off the boat and looking for lodgings and maybe a bit more...wink, wink! But by the time me and my mad crowd started going, the L8 clubs had become somewhere you would only go to finish off the night, never to start it. The Yoruba, the Nigerian, the Somali Club, the Pink Flamingo, Stanley House, Dutch Eddies, Wilkies, the Ghana and, of course, the Ibo and the Gladray were the most popular with young and older punters. The Ibo had a manager called Mr

Ankarah, and he never ever seemed to smile. He'd see you walk in and say in a loud voice, 'Pay at the door. Sign the book… Sign the book!' – at which point me and my friends would shit ourselves and start scrawling anything in the book just so he wouldn't shout at us anymore.

Inside the Ibo it was ever so slightly sleazy and some of the men and women sitting around were letting their hands do a tad too much fondling for the room of a nightclub. Some of the older prostitutes – who stood up on Lime Street and certain streets in Toxteth – liked to hang out at these clubs, trying to pick up the older gents who were visiting the city, and/or the country. One thing I knew about the women who were turning a trick back then, most of the money they made went straight back to their families to pay for their kids' clothes and to put food on the table. A life choice, it was in no way like the drugged-up girls you get going on the game nowadays, a lot of whom are forced into 'the life' by ruthless pimps.

The Gladray Club was on Upper Parliament Street and took its name from its founders. Two sisters, Gladys and Rachel, ran the club and made it famous as Liverpool's first strip club. The first time I ever walked in there, one of the sisters looked me up and down, like she was trying to suss out if I was old enough to be in there. The Gladray was a strip club in the daytime, a kind of family club in the late afternoon, and then a nightclub in the night-time, so it was really unique. But after having one of the sisters – I don't know if it was Gladys or Rachel – eyeballing me for half the night, I didn't go back.

She probably saw my flat chest and thought I was a lad trying to pass myself off as a girl!

I'll always remember the first thing I noticed when I walked in was the neckties hanging over the bar. There were lots of them, and most had been cut in half. I was later told by my pisshead friend Janet – I hope she's not reading this, I love you really, girl! Where was I? Oh yes, Janet said the ties over the bar had been cut off the necks of the men who'd been wearing them; hacked off with a pair of scissors, just because the sisters didn't want anyone looking all haughty and stuck-up. Now, I'm not sure how true that is, but it would explain it.

As well as all these Caribbean, Disco and RnB clubs, there was a complete range of alternative sub-culture clubs. The places where you would find punks spitting at each other while they jumped around the dance floor; Rockabilly clubs were still about, having opened their doors in the fifties, then there were the New Romantic clubs springing up in the late seventies that seemed to mix with the emerging Goth scenes, having the same appeal to the guys who liked to wear make-up, not because they were gay, but because it was a style. Followers of these musical scenes had their own look and fashion sense that stood out more than most other styles. Myself and my friends tried each and every one of those styles, moving from grimy punk to big-shouldered Duran Duran wannabes, although we soon grew weary of trying to be radical and changed back to the RnB and disco styles of the day.

CHAPTER EIGHT

DANGEROUS TIMES

B eing a kid in the sixties and seventies was fraught with danger and a serious risk to our health, if not our lives. If a bunch of you weren't hanging wrecking-ball style, some thirty feet in the air from an Otterspool Park swing rope, or falling from a German wall in the cathedral grounds, or being terrorised by thoughts of Spring-Heeled Jack, then you were most likely to be dodging the fists or boots of adults who could give you a dig if they thought you were being cheeky. Most of these adults were complete strangers or people other than your parents, with whom you interacted in everyday life. This happened to me and me mates so many times we lost count. It was usually on buses where, being a confined space, you couldn't move out of the way of a dig or a slap quickly enough. Whenever it did happen to you or one of your gang – let's say a man or woman heard you swear and they gave you a clip round the ear or a kick – instead of kicking off with a mouthful of abuse, calling the police or attacking the person (like the kids do nowadays), we would all just laugh at the mate who got a dig or a slap…at least we would until the adult in question turned their attention to us.

It was the same thing in school – when a teacher would catch you being noisy, they could give you a dig. An old favourite was for the teacher to hit the kid with a well-aimed wooden chalkboard rubber. The teachers were expert at this and you would swear one or two of them, whose aim was so accurate, could have started an Olympic sport. Many times, I saw a chalk-board rubber lobbed from one end of the class to the other to make perfect contact with the head of a kid who was pissing around, mid-lesson. Most of the time I was that kid. Yes, violence towards kids had the government stamp of approval in the sixties and seventies and you didn't dare complain. If you were hit by a teacher's chalkboard projectile and you went home to tell your mam or dad, they would give you a beating and say, 'Well, you must have been being cheeky for the teacher to have hit you in the first place!'

Other than adults throwing things at you, there were those few who fired guns at you. 'Guns?' I hear you gasp, disbelievingly. Yes, guns – shot and air, gun and pistol. Freshfields, near Formby, was the first place I encountered gun terror. Myself and three friends, my mate Queeny (so-called for no known reason whatsoever), Jean (my bessie mate at the time) and Sandra, or 'Sand', who was really a mate of Jean's, which meant we had to let her tag along even though she always smelled a bit off, like she'd peed herself a week ago and hadn't bothered to change her knicks. Anyway, we all decided to go to Freshfields as we were sagging (bunking off) school and hanging around Lime Street station, looking to bunk on a train. Then Sandra, who always had her eyes peeled to the ground, spotted a five-pound note stuck near to one of the phone booths. So we decided we didn't have to bunk and instead loaded up with sweets and paid for tickets to Freshfields.

Now, Freshfields – for those of you who don't know – was a place every Liverpool family went to when they wanted to take their kids for a day out, but had grown bored with New Brighton and didn't have enough money for the fairground rides in Southport. And there were no shops or ice-cream vans in Freshfields so it really was a cheap day out. What Freshfields did have was squirrels – little red squirrels – and a forest of pine trees. At the end of the pines were sand dunes and then a beach that could take you to Crosby Beach if you took a sharp left, and Southport Beach if you turned right. That day, after finding the money and eating too many sweets, we were all hyper as fuck. When we spilled out into Freshfields, we were also loaded up with ciggies and matches – I think we had ten Gold Bond cigarettes between us (Gold Bond were the pre-Benson & Hedges ciggies and you could buy them in fives or tens).

Me, Jean and Queeny immediately ran off into the woods and found a place to sit and smoke ourselves sick. The truth was that only Queeny enjoyed smoking, but me and Jean felt peer-pressured to follow her example. Pissy Sandra didn't seem to feel peer pressured at all – I mean, she didn't even feel pressured into changing her flamin' knickers, for God's sake – and when she caught up with us, sat staring at us smoking and giving us daggers right up to the point where I got pissed off and fronted her.

'Who ya staring at?' I said.

'Don't know, they don't label shit,' she retorted.

Needless to say, I flew at her, but Jean stopped me. So, back to the 'danger for kids' part of my story… In Freshfields, there were lots of farmers' fields with only small hedges protecting their cabbages, lettuces, sprouts and beetroots from being nicked by little shites like me and me mates – and pissy Sandra too. To cut a long story short, we decided our mams would like some of whatever was growing in the first field we came across, so they could serve it up with our tea that evening. So, Jean jumped into the field, then me, but Queeny fell into the hedge and cut her leg. Then suddenly, pissy Sandra jumps over the hedge and runs off across the field like a fuckin' nutter, and for some unknown reason we all ran after her. I suppose it's because in all truth, kids will always follow other kids if they start running for no reason, just in case they've spotted something the others haven't.

So, we ran right across the field, kicking what I think were cabbages or lettuce from our path, but then stopped and started laughing our heads off while gasping for breath. And for about ten, maybe fifteen seconds, I found myself actually liking pissy Sandra. Then we heard…boom! We all screamed at the same time and automatically ducked. When we looked up, I was the first to spot a farmer, standing in the field with a real gun aimed right at us. I was gone – and I mean gone too – across the field, with the others following close behind. There have never been four schoolgirls who have crossed a cabbage field that fast, you could probably bet money on it. We were over the fence in one synchronised leap, disappearing into the woods and darting in and out of trees, with the farmer laughing and shouting all manner of swear words in the distance. Half of them I hadn't even heard before and I lived in L8!

We kept that little incident to ourselves as we knew if we told our parents what had happened, they'd have said, 'You shouldn't have been robbing the man's vegetables, you little thief!' And if we'd told the police that a farmer shot at us in his field, they'd have just arrested us and let the farmer press charges. It turned out the farmer wasn't trying to kill us after all and what he'd shot us with was rock salt or some kind of pepper kernels, according to Jean's mam. The coolest mam you could wish for, she was the only one out of our parents we told. She said she'd have given the farmer a punch in the teeth if she'd have been with us.

Jean's mam was great and totally on a kid's level. I think she was more understanding because she had been bullied and beaten as a child and all of the bullying and beatings had come from adults so she didn't think every time a kid got hit by an adult that it automatically meant it must have been the kid's fault. She was the only adult we'd tell whenever we got shot at on our way back from stealing biscuits from the biscuit factory in Edge Hill. Although she wasn't fully on side because we kept going back, so it was our own friggin' faults.

The biscuit factory was called Crawford's and we didn't actually steal biscuits, that is to say we didn't go into the factory and take the biscuits they were going to sell to the shops. What we did do was climb into the skip at the back of the factory and steal the broken biscuits they were throwing away. Most of the ladies who worked in the factory used to see us scrambling into the skips and sometimes they would come out with bags of unbroken biscuits and give them to us. We would be so happy and dead polite, thanking the ladies over and over again. But even when none of them were about and we had to make do with the reject biscuits, we were still happy as Larry because you always found the mutant biscuits in the skip.

'What!' we'd shout when one of us discovered a mutant-sized banana-flavoured wafer. We'd say it was mutated because it was huge as it had been rejected before it had been cut into little wafers. Other times, we found a giant chocolate United biscuit, which was really lots of normal-sized United biscuits melted into one. The worst thing me and me mates found – which at the time we all thought was the best thing ever – was a large block of what we thought was pink cream biscuit filling, the type you would find sandwiched in a strawberry cream biscuit. We leapt from the skip – I think the girl who found it was called Sue – and she and the rest of us climbed through the broken wall at the back of the factory and headed off down the railway tracks. I remember how excited we were, looking at the pink cream: it was like we were dogs in the dog pound, waiting to be fed our first ever juicy steak.

About halfway down the track, and clear of the factory, we stopped and Sue broke pieces off the cream for each of us to sample. Automatically, and like only kids do, we all waited to taste it at the same time. One, two, three…we bit into the cream. 'Argh!' we grimaced. It wasn't pink cream after all, but pink lard! Some kind of big lump of lard or something used to cook biscuits in that had been coloured by food colouring, like your whites getting stained in the wash. Each of us stood with our teeth almost glued together as we stared at each other in horror. Then we spat; one girl vomited, and the rest of us scrambled to find twigs or anything else we could use to scrape the lard from our teeth. But there really wasn't much we could do except hope that the warmth of our mouths would eventually melt the lard and allow us to spit it out. The day was also marred by the appearance of 'Fat Shit' –the guy who drove a small spotter train along the railway, trying to catch kids playing on the railway tracks. Looking back, as an adult on Fat Shit and his spotter train, I thank God that he was there. If he hadn't been, the amount of kids knocked down and killed by trains would have been in mad numbers, although of course to us at that time Fat Shit was just some sadistic shit who liked shooting kids with an air rifle from the back of his spotter train.

Now, I don't know if Fat Shit was an actual person someone had seen and named while getting shot at, but the only people I ever saw driving the spotter trains were small fellas, who even

I could have had a go at fighting if they hadn't been armed and fuckin' dangerous. The slow walk back along the train tracks that day was bleedin' horrible. Shoulders slumped, mouths plastered with pink lard and no biscuits because everyone felt too sick to want to eat any. Then all of a sudden we hear the familiar whizz noise of a pellet just missing our heads. Next thing, one of us gets hit with a pellet and screams. We turn around and there's the spotter train heading towards us. 'Leggit!' I shout as we take off, but one of the girls – I can't remember her name, but she had a shock of ginger hair and braces on her teeth – decides to try and hide by jumping into a bush full of stinging nettles. The rest of us made it off the rail tracks without further pellet wounds, but the ginger-haired girl ended up being rubbed down with dock leaves for the rest of the day.

I suppose the all-time most dangerous things for kids of my day were other kids. I've already mentioned the kids piling onto the swing in Otterspool Park and endangering the lives of the ones already swinging on it – well, that kind of danger came to us on a daily basis. If me and my friends went out of the area we lived in when we were little, then we stood a good chance of getting beaten up by kids who lived in that area. It didn't matter what race or how big or small you were, there would always be some gang of kids who would shout, 'Hey, girl/lad! Whereabouts you from?' and as soon as you heard those words – unless you could say you were from that area – then you were in shit street. No matter what you answered with, the kid who shouted would either twist your words...

'I'm from Toxteth!'

'And that makes you think you're harder than me?'

Or they would come up with some bullshit claim...

'I'm from Toxteth!'

'Toxteth? You're the ones that jumped my brother!'

So, any time a kid in an unfamiliar area of the city shouted over to us we would just leg it. And once we did, the kids would always come after us. Most of the time we'd end up in a shop, hoping the owner would let us stay until the gang tired of telling us how badly they were going to kick the crap out of us and just went away. I still remember standing with three mates in a shop and pretending we were browsing for sweets for almost an hour, and then getting stroppy with the shop owner, while promising, 'We're gonna buy something in a minute, God!'

When we were kids, Liverpool had no-go areas all over the city, but as we grew up, we realised the no-go areas depended on where you lived. What I'm trying to say is that every area you didn't live in was at some time considered a no-go area. Thinking back, I'm shocked at the sheer number of times kids from other areas would want to beat us up when they didn't even know who we were, or if we were nice kids or arseholes.

In 1979 a film came on at the cinema called *The Warriors*. It told the story of a New York City gang trapped on the far side of the city, who have to make it all the way home through the territory of lots of rival gangs, all out to kill them. Okay, we didn't have gangs of kids looking to kill us, but every now and then we would find ourselves having to make it home through the city and coming across gangs who were bored and wanting to relieve that boredom by punching our faces really hard.

I remember a 'Warrior' moment when there was only me and my friend Maureen, and a girl we'll call Donna. We got the bus across the city to see Donna's boyfriend because she said he had lots of nice mates. None of us had the bus fare to get back home, but Donna's boyfriend had a job and was seventeen – even though she was only thirteen… dodgy! – and he would pay our fare back. We got to Donna's boyfriend's house and he'd gone to stay in Wiltshire with his dad. It was only late afternoon, but it was winter so it was pitch-black. We had to walk all the way back, because unlike now, we never had mobile phones to call our parents. I remember it taking us ages getting back because every time we saw a group of kids on a corner or sitting on a wall, we ducked out of sight and had to leg it back the way we came, just in case one of them shouted that famous line, 'Hey, girl! Whereabouts you from?'

I can still remember how relieved I felt when we finally got on to Parliament Street and started walking up towards home, and I can also remember the sinking feeling in my stomach when I heard a kid's voice shout, 'Get 'em!'

Maureen shouted, 'Run!' almost at the same time as the lad shouted – I think that's because we were all on edge and ready to bolt at the first excuse. As we were running as fast as we could run, I turned to look at who was chasing us. It was a huge gang of random kids: white, black, girls, lads, fat, thin, tall and small. In other words, there was no reason for them to want to pick on us, they were just being little bastards who were bored and wanted to terrorise someone. Poor Donna, she was heaving and crying as we were running and, just like one of the guys in the *Warriors* film, she suddenly said, 'I…I can't run any more!'

'Bloody hell!' I said.

Maureen said, 'Leave her!'

Now, Maureen could be a bit of a bitch when she wanted. I couldn't leave Donna, even though I was a kid and I should have been able to, because that's what kids do – it's their right. Instead I shouted, 'Get in Swainee's!'

Swainee's was the slang name for the Swainbanks Antique Furniture shop that was housed in the Rialto building at 90–94 Upper Parliament Street. The Rialto was massive and as ornate a building as you could get, having once been a prestigious theatre that was covered in white tiles, with a large central balcony, stone columns and two domed towers. Me and lots of the kids in the area used to go into Swainee's to mess about and hide behind the furniture that was sometimes piled high to the ceiling. So me, Maureen and Donna legged it into Swainee's and through the twists and turns, past the furniture and then…

'Out!' we heard. 'Now!' It was Mr Swainbank, who was sitting on a dark blue, velvet-covered chair amongst a load of other chairs – he must have been taking a rest from work and we'd disturbed him. He stood up: 'Come on, out! All of you!' The kids who were chasing us turned to leave without a fuss because they knew we were cornered and they could get us as soon as we stepped outside. Then Mr Swainbank did something really nice. He must have noticed that we looked scared and that Donna was out of breath and sobbing because he added, 'Oi! Youse three can stay!'

I swear to God I have never felt more relieved from that day to this. Mr Swainbank had one of his employees chase the kids out and threaten them with the police if they didn't clear off, and then he let us stay in the shop until we felt sure they had gone. What a completely nice man! 'Thank you, Mr Swainbank,' we kept saying every time he said anything to us. We walked around the shop for nearly an hour to make sure those little bastards had sodded off, and I can still remember to this day the smell of old furniture and beeswax polish mixed with the smell from the paraffin lamps.

We made it home safe and sound that day, although Donna's mam didn't let her go to see her so-called boyfriend again because the silly cow told her everything that had happened. I remember her mam was none too keen on us hanging around with her daughter after that day, even though it was Donna's fault we got stranded in the first place.

After that, I went back to Swainee's lots of times. I think it became my Switzerland, my neutral zone where I felt safe, because Mr Swainbank kept us all safe that day. He never said another word to me or Maureen after the day we ran in there seeking sanctuary, but every now and then he would give us a little smile when he saw us hanging around the shop.

We never saw the gang that chased us after that, and me and Maureen never ever went out of the area without having the bus fare to get back home. As I said, when I was a kid life could be dangerous, so thank God for adults like Mr Swainbank, who cared enough to rescue us from danger.

The Rialto/Swainbanks was a true Liverpool landmark, which made it all the more of a shame when the building was razed by arsonists during the Toxteth riots of July 1981.

CHAPTER NINE

CHINATOWN

Some time ago, while rehearsing for a well-known TV show, I bumped into an actor colleague and we got talking about his city of birth and my city, Liverpool. Some way into the conversation – which was dull as hell because he had the most monotone voice you could ever hear and was cocksure that every comment he made was gospel – he suddenly made the statement that Liverpool has no real culture. At which point my eyes changed from being half-asleep to propping wide open.

'No culture?' I said. 'You cheeky bugger!'

The actor seemed a little shocked by my outburst, which I explained later was due to the fact he'd bored me half to sleep and I always wake up pissed off when I've been asleep. I did calm down eventually and then took pleasure in correcting his obvious lack of knowledge.

In Liverpool, the culture abounds, whether it's the north end of the city, which has many cultures – the Irish and Scottish heritages being the first that spring to mind – or the south of the city, an area rich in cultures from across the globe. I told him that Liverpool's Chinatown was the oldest one in Europe, with the biggest Chinese arch outside of mainland China. Good enough, he did listen and ask questions and, by the end of the day, I'd educated him and he was genuinely interested in seeing the places I'd mentioned in Liverpool, which I insisted he should, especially with him being an actor as our city has turned out some of the greatest entertainers and actors to date.

Anyway, just talking about Chinatown rekindled the memories of playing there as a child, and of the friends who lived there. I suppose many of my best friends were from all races and cultures because I lived in the heart of the multicultural part of the city, and one of these friends, Sarah, was Chinese. Unlike the other kids I hung around with, she could speak two languages. Now, although my other mates might have had parents for whom English was a second language, those kids hadn't bothered to learn their parents' mother tongue at all. You see, no one had encouraged them to do so, because their parents thought that speaking another language might alienate their kids from the barely English-speaking Scouse kids they were hanging out with at the time. Sarah had, and like the whole of the Chinese community, spoke Chinese on a regular basis, but never in front of us. No way, that was taboo! I remember us actually trying to bribe Sarah with money, dinner tickets, sweets, toys, anything just so she would say one sentence in Chinese with the proper accent, but no way would she do it. So, we changed it to just saying one word instead, but nope, not one word would she say.

Aargh, it was so frustrating! If it was me and I could speak Chinese or any other language, I'd have been in my element – showing off, speaking it without any prompt or bribe. And if someone was giving me money or sweets to talk, I'd never shut up. But me mate Sarah was steadfast and never swayed to temptation. I think I secretly admired her for that, but it was still bloody frustrating. The only time I heard her speak Chinese (or Mandarin, to be exact) was when she had no choice because I'd called to hers when her gran was home – who was first-generation Chinese and didn't speak any English – and she started talking to Sarah, and Sarah had to answer her.

I swear I have never seen anyone turn around and look at me so paranoid. It was like she'd just revealed where Lord Lucan was hiding. But I just grinned because I'd finally heard her speak Chinese and hadn't had to pay her any money or give her my sweets.

I loved hanging out in Chinatown. It was a strange place for a kid because it always seemed empty except for the restaurant-goers and the people who worked there. You never seemed to see Chinese families just hanging around, and you never ever saw a gang of Chinese kids hanging around on a street corner or playing in the parks. However, on a Sunday, the whole of Chinatown came alive with families just shopping and hanging about. My mate said it was because Chinese families all work hard as a community and that's why you only ever see them on a Sunday, which was like their day off.

There was one part of the Chinatown community that never seemed to take a day off and that was the gambling houses. As we played in Chinatown, we could always hear the sound of the Mahjong tiles hitting the gambling tables in the casinos above the restaurants, although at the time we didn't have a clue what was making the strange noise. I used to be happiest in Chinatown when Sarah's family would feed me whenever I was visiting her house, and although they didn't have a restaurant, their food tasted nicer than any I'd ever tasted.

In our house the food was okay and it filled us up, but it wasn't full of exotic spices and there was very little variety. My dad used to con us into thinking we had a lot more choices than we actually did. He used to say, 'Do you want chips and egg and beans, or, beans and chips and egg, or do you want chips and beans with an egg on top... which one?' You'd be thinking, it's the same fuckin' meal! But for some reason we'd stand there puzzling our heads, trying to make a choice. And what made it even more ridiculous was there was always one choice that sounded better than the others. We must have been bloody thick! I used to love egg, chips and beans, no matter what order they came in, but my favourite meal was sausage, egg, chips and beans, which we hardly ever got. Back then, if I was on death row, my last meal would have been sausage, egg, chips and beans...in that order, although I might have been tempted to change it for one of Sarah's Chinese meals.

It was Sarah's house where I first tasted prawns, but I didn't like them because someone had told me they were like insects from the sea, and although they tasted lovely, I could hardly swallow them for thinking about eating bugs. I remember meeting Sarah's mum for the first time and her mentioning that Sarah's older sister had been in a dead famous film in the late fifties. The film was called *The Inn of the Sixth Happiness* and it starred one of Hollywood's biggest stars, Ingrid Bergman, as real-life missionary Gladys Aylward. I was amazed that the people who made all of those big movies in Hollywood had heard of Linda, Sarah's sister, and had come all the way over here to put her in one of their movies. Then I found out that Linda wasn't so special, as they had recruited half the kids in Chinatown to be in the movie because it was supposed to be set in China, but they filmed it in Portmeirion in Wales. It turned out the nearest Chinese community at that time was Liverpool's Chinatown, and they needed lots of Chinese kids as extras in the film. Linda said that she spoke to Ingrid Bergman lots of times and she had been one of her favourite kids on the set.

I remember having to wait for almost three years for that film to come on TV. Nowadays, I would have been streaming it the same day. When it did come on the TV, me and my mam were all excited because other Chinese kids from where we lived in Windsor Gardens had also been recruited to be in the film. We spent the whole film trying to spot Linda and the other Chinese kids. I spotted Linda, but she looked loads younger, and my mam thought she spotted one of Mrs Ching's kids (she was our neighbour), but wasn't sure. After that, whenever I was with any mates and saw Linda, I would tell them what film she was in and boast that I had been in her mum's house lots of times, eating sea insects. Not that me eating sea insects ever made me mates jealous, but they were slightly envious that I'd been in the same house as a movie star.

The big event in every Chinatown in any city is Chinese New Year and, each year, I couldn't wait to go and celebrate with my mates. I was born on 28 September 1958 and up until I started hanging around my Chinese mates, I was a Libra birthsign only. Then they told me I was also a Dog – that's the Chinese birthsign dog. Fuck me, what an awful sign! I actually found myself wishing I was a rat at least. But then Sarah's nan explained that being a dog didn't mean I was prone to sniffing people's arseholes, it meant I was caring, supportive, loyal, I liked to plan, and I was intelligent – her nan changed her mind about the latter once she got to know me!

I always felt a little bit privileged to hang around with my Chinese mates. I don't know why, it's not like I knew how old their culture was or anything like that. I just think it might have been because they were part of a close-knit community and kept themselves to themselves, so I felt a bit special because they must have thought a lot of me to bring me into that community as a friend. Don't get me wrong, they weren't snobby, and they didn't see themselves as any better than the other girls, but their culture was more focused and ordered, and they were expected to help with family matters and they never refused to do what they were told by an elder in the family. We, on the other hand, would be constantly looking for ways of avoiding everything and anything we were told to do – I suppose you have to be born into a culture to respect its ways.

CHAPTER TEN

POWERLESS

Along with The Beatles and space exploration, power cuts were very popular in the 1960s and 70s. For those of you who were born post-1980, you probably won't have heard of these events, so let me try and enlighten you. Imagine you're sitting there minding your own business, having dinner, watching the telly or playing games, and the next minute you're in total blackness. Or imagine you're walking along at night and the street is illuminated by street lamps, then the next minute you're in total darkness. In both cases you are now in the middle of a blackout. The country's electricity network had been a mechanical disaster in the 1960s and a target for industrial action in the 70s. In December 1970 all of the hospitals in Liverpool had to resort to using batteries and in some cases candles during a major strike. Then, in 1972, the situation went from bad to worse when Edward Heath went head to head with the unions, kicking off the miners' strike over pay. The miners were demanding a £9 a week pay rise, and until they got it the power could be cut off without any warning whatsoever. They stood their ground; got their pay increase and the lights came back on. And although the increase wasn't the exact amount they'd asked for it still put them amongst the highest paid in the working classes.

In 1978–79, someone discovered oil and gas in the North Sea and that ended the most of the blackouts.

To me, blackouts were exciting because I was a kid, and kids revel in the unusual and unpredictable. However, a sudden blackout must have been a head-wrecker for parents when halfway through the cooking, your oven goes off. There was never any warning from the local government either. One minute you were there watching *Corrie*, next thing you hear the familiar dull click of the shutdown and everything turns black.

We'd all start screaming and laughing with excitement while my mam would start shouting commands:

'Get the candles!'

'Where are they?'

'You know where they are! Where they always are, under the stairs!'

'Where are the stairs?'

'God almighty, give me strength!'

Every family had their own stash of candles and they all had their own chosen place where they kept them. Ours were under the stairs in our house and before that they were in the airing cupboard in Nan's flat. Once you found the candles – which was no easy task as you still had to fight your brothers and sisters in the pitch-black so you could get to them first – you could never find the matches. There was no regular place to keep them back then as there were a number of uses for them so they tended to get moved about a lot.

Candles lit, you had to make your own amusement. Mam would light our emergency candles and tell us all ghost stories, which made us terrified before we went to bed. She wasn't always the best at making up ghost stories so she'd just include whatever horror films she could remember and use the names of the creatures and the characters from the film. However, half the time she'd get the creatures' names mixed up with the names of the actors who were playing the parts. So we'd have a story about a guy called Christopher Lee, who was this fella who had to climb in through your bedroom window to bite people because he was always hungry, but you first had to invite him in through the bedroom window before he could bite you, which never made any sense in my head. Or some guy called Boris, who was made from spare parts, with a square head, bolts in his neck and had a thing for electricity. One of the stories I remember she told us had a guy called Lon Chaney, who had a son called Junior, who got a furry face whenever the moon was full. This one was my favourite, but it also scared me the most. Every full moon I used to imagine the furry-faced man climbing up to the window and hearing his howl, and me, still half asleep, thinking he was a stray cat or something because in the dark I could only make out the fur; then I open the window and he chews my head off. I remember my brother was so impressed by Mam's story about the guy Boris, who must have got his square head fixed by wrapping himself in Mummy bandages, he cut up her best sheet, trying to be the Mummy for Halloween, and my mam battered him.

I suppose the people who loved the blackouts even more than us kids were the opportunists. These guys used to pray for blackouts, and as soon as one struck, they would load up whatever gear they had and set off into town. The streets were as black as pitch, especially if there was no moon in the sky, because all the street lamps would be off. These 'opportunists' or thieving shits as they were known, would actually go into town, throw bricks through department store windows and steal the dummies with the clothes on from out of the window. And because there was no electric the alarms wouldn't go off, so if the smashing of the window was done carefully enough and without too much sound, the thieves could stay there until the window was cleared out and then move on to the next store.

You could always tell who these opportunists were because the next day they'd be knocking on your door, trying to flog the stuff they'd stolen. Good enough, my mam, Dad and Nan would never buy the hooky stuff off them: 'You wanna try further down, lad,' Dad would say to them, pointing a finger in the direction of the next tenements. Mam and Nan wouldn't be as calm though: 'Don't you come knocking here with your knock-off stuff! Go on with ya!' was their reply to 'Got some lovely dresses here, love.' You could always tell what neighbour had bought the hooky clothes because you'd see them prancing around without occasion, showing off their new dress or handbag, or bragging about the new television set their husband saved up and bought from the local telly shop. I think they were just getting back-up on their stories in case the police called.

So, as you see, the blackouts weren't just about the electricity going off, they were an opportunity for thieves to make a few quid, and for mothers to scare the shit out of their kids with ghost stories. In a weird way they also seemed to bring families closer together...well, with the exception of those families whose dad was off robbing showroom dummies. It wasn't like we had too many distractions like we have now, laptops, tablets, mobile phones, etc., but the ones we did have were set on pause by the blackouts and we almost, you might say, went back to an ancient way of doing things: sitting around a fireplace, telling stories.

CHAPTER ELEVEN

THE CHARACTERS

There were lots of larger-than-life characters in Liverpool when I was growing up, and Liverpool 8 had more than its fair share. The first one that pops into my head is Shadow. Now, Shadow was a street trader and a huge figure of a man, either of Caribbean or African descent. A gentle giant, best known for his array of costumes in the Merseyside Caribbean Carnival, he appeared in full drag on his carnival float as Britannia on a giant fifty-pence piece. He won first place that year. Shadow walked around Liverpool 8 selling his beads, carvings and other wares, and he was always humming and singing.

I remember him laughing with me one year at the carnival. He was trailing behind the floats, dressed as Quasimodo, from *The Hunchback of Notre Dame*. I was showing off and, at the time, I didn't know who he was dressed up as. 'Who are you supposed to be?' I shouted. He laughed and shouted back at me, 'I'll give you a clue! This thing on my back ain't a heat spot!' Both of us laughed as he wandered off, ringing his bell.

Another character from the area was nicknamed Froggy. An old, slim black man, I wasn't really sure where he was from, the Caribbean or Africa, but he was always running. He was really old, but he would sprint past us kids with his shiny shoes that any other person would have slipped over in, and he'd always smile as he zipped by. There was a large man called Shablo – forgive my spelling – and he used to say three words to you whenever he walked past, 'One time, Shablow!', and then he would go off on his way.

Then there was Mr Coffee from the church, who used to ask us if we loved Jesus, and Mr Myers the debt collector, who we used to think was our uncle and always walked like he was creeping and didn't want his footsteps heard. There was also the Hop Skip and Jump Man, who I think would be diagnosed with some kind of autism nowadays, but back then we just thought he was a little nuts and eccentric. He used to be walking along and then he would suddenly stop in the middle of the pavement. After a hop, skip and jump, making sure he avoided the grouting in between certain paving stones, he'd continue on his way as normal.

The man who delivered our coal was another funny character. His name was Uncle Pip – even though he wasn't an uncle of ours – but we called him that because he did the same kind of silly things your uncle might do when carrying out mundane work. Every time he'd throw the coal down the chute, he would scream and wail out loud like a strangled cat, then he'd turn to us kids and say the same thing every time, 'Uh sorry, I got your cat.'

The man who delivered the *Liverpool Echo* on his bike was another standout character. Not because he did anything strange or unusual, unlike the others I've mentioned, it was more what we used to do whenever we saw him cycling past. These days you only get the static – standing on a street corner – *Echo* man, but when we were kids, the *Echo* man was on a bike and he'd travel all over the city, shouting, '*Echo!*' We used to be little bastards and shout, 'What do ya wipe your arse on?' and he'd shout, '*Echo!*'

There were two other characters who I remember from back in the day that happened to be in the same profession as each other and had shops that stood around four shops apart from each other. These were the hair barbers, Mr Pee-Wee, and Mr Mac. Pee-Wee was an old Trinidadian gent, who sat outside his barber's shop on Granby Street playing his guitar and singing to the ladies that walked by. He was said to be a demon with a cut-throat razor, giving the closest shave in the Northwest. Mac was a Caribbean man, who always wore a flat cap and chose to hum rather than sing throughout the day.

Being a girl, I never had my hair cut by either barber until the day I decided to cut my hair myself. I wanted to go to a new hairdresser's that had opened near to where I lived because a friend of mine – a friend whose parents were well off – had been and got her hair styled there. I was only six or seven years old at the time so there was no way Mam and Dad were sending me to a stylist. So, in an act of rebellion, I decided to cut my own hair and made a horrible mess of it. My dad decided to teach me a lesson by taking me to Pee-Wee's barber shop to straighten my hair out. I remember Pee-Wee was sitting outside his shop, singing, but Dad spotted that he'd also been having a few cans of beer, so he said his hellos and then we went to Mac's instead.

I remember walking in ahead of Dad and seeing the cigarette smoke pour out of the door like a cloud. Inside, there were men whose origins were from all over the Caribbean. Seeing that the shop was crowded made me believe I'd dodged a bullet because there was no way my dad would want to go in when there were so many men waiting ahead of us. It turned out these men were regulars, who sat in the barber's shop every day, just chatting and socialising. Mac called my dad and me forward, Dad muttered something to Mac, something I didn't hear, because I was too focused on what looked like two prostitutes stood to one side, grinning straight at me. I'll never forget that one of them had curly red hair and looked like the actor Charlie Drake, and the other was tall and elegant-looking, but she had rough-looking skin and yellow teeth. Mac turned the barber's chair around to face me. He put a plank of wood across the chair handles and had Dad lift me up and sit me on it. Then he put a nylon robe around my shoulders, a robe still covered with hair from previous customer cuts.

My dad sat down and talked to the men while Mac started cutting my hair. I will never forget that he decided halfway through my cut to eat a piece of some kind of pie that slowly ended up in my hair. I just sat there, stiff as the plank I was sitting on, staring into the mirror without moving or saying a word, deliberately avoiding eye contact with the prozzies, who, in all fairness, were only trying to be nice to a little girl. Mac straightened up my hair, but he had to take a lot off, which made me look like a tomboy for a few weeks. This thrilled me mates as they constantly compared me to any footballer with short hair. From that day on, I never attempted to do something as stupid as cutting my own hair.

CHAPTER TWELVE

THE FOOTY

For most of my family and nigh on half the population of Liverpool, the highlight of the 1960s football calendar began with Liverpool winning 3–2 against Arsenal in 1964 after a seventeen-year wait. It was the first match ever to be shown on the BBC's *Match of the Day* programme and the city went wild, but not nearly as wild as when Liverpool won the FA Cup Final on 1 May 1965. The match was against Leeds United, with a final score of Liverpool 2, Leeds United 1. Roger Hunt scored the first goal heading it home in the ninety-third minute and Ian St John scored the second with a diving header in the one-hundreth and eleventh minute.

People were chanting on the tenement landings like they were there live at the match. Houses, shops and businesses displayed red scarves and flags with the Liverpool crest. And even if you didn't want to celebrate, your parents made sure you did. I was dragged into town by my mam to stand outside

Lewis's department store to see Liverpool FC's homecoming. Although I was more than happy to stand in this very same spot when watching Santa's Parade at Christmas time, now I had to stand here and watch a bunch of men from a sport I didn't even follow. I was sulking all the way into town and by the time I arrived at Lewis's, I'd added huffing and whining to the mix.

After standing around for what seemed like ages with my mam excitedly waving a scarf, the crowd suddenly went crazy. The police were the first thing I saw as they tried to clear the road so that the players' bus could get through at a steady pace. No such luck, the bus moved at a snail's pace because the crowds could not be moved. While we waited for that bus to finally get to whereabouts me and Mam were standing, I remember looking at the gleeful look on my mam's face. I remember thinking I hadn't seen her look that happy in ages. You have to understand that at that time in Liverpool the only people having a stress-free time were the flippin' Beatles! Everyone else was fighting to put clothes on their backs and food on the table. So to see my mam's face genuinely free of life's wearing and tearing, if only for that fleeting moment, was a memory I'll always cherish. And from that moment on, looking at my mam and all of the faces that surrounded me that were full of joy, I was hooked! I started yelling and waving as the bus ambled its way towards the flower beds outside Lewis's. Then Mam smiled at me and gave me a hug – I think she was happy that I'd stopped sulking and we were sharing a special and historic moment together. This made me yell with even more enthusiasm and by the time the parade reached us, my voice was almost gone.

I remember being amazed that I could actually see the team players on an open-top bus driving through swathes of fans that blocked the main road and every street leading onto it. Then Mam started pointing with excitement and she lifted me up to show me three men on the bus. 'That's Roger Hunt,' she said proudly, pointing, 'he scored the first goal.' I remember not being sure which player she was pointing at. 'And that's St John, he scored the second.' Mam was pointing at a very happy man, who was chanting back at the chanting crowd. At that moment she almost lost her mind as she pointed and yelled, 'Shankly! That's Bill Shankly, girl!' But I didn't look where my mam was pointing, instead I smiled and watched the excitement on her face as tears of pride welled up in her eyes. Up to that moment I had only noticed her cry the one time, on the day she got all her hair cut off and sold it because our family had no money. My dad loved Mam's locks and when he saw they were gone, he cried, and she cried with him. But these tears were happy ones.

Every shop, store or house window was crammed tight that day with people waving and screaming as the bus passed by. Even the Blue-noses (Evertonians) were giving them a wave because the win gave everybody a renewed pride in our city.

There were lots of street parties that seemed to go on forever. Bunting was strewn across the front of every house and from one side of the road to the other. Tables were gathered from houses, churches and pubs and joined together in the middle of the roads, like they were set up for a Viking feast. Sandwiches, butties, fruit juice, cakes, sausage rolls –my favourite, along with jelly and custard – there was trifle and fizzy pop, so much of it you made yourself sick, and when you felt a bit better and your stomach had settled, you drank lots more.

Everybody had little flags and waved them as they stuffed their faces and sang, danced and got pissed – if you were an adult or a teen sneaking some beer from the stacks of beer crates that were everywhere. The local drunks were out in force, and probably for the first time in as long as they could remember, they had a genuine excuse to get pissed. There was one man called Docker, who lived in our tenement block and he was so drunk and happy to have seen Liverpool win, he was chucking his money about like he was Rockefeller himself. He threw pockets of change at us kids and we all scrambled over each other to get at them. Docker's wife, Barbara, almost had a fit when she saw him tossing away the rent money – 'Get that money back in, you drunken bugger!' In truth, whenever there was any kind of celebration, Docker would appear, pissed as a navvy, throwing money at us kids. And when he wasn't wasting the rent money on us, he was getting stopped by the police for being drunk. But the police knew him well and so they didn't really arrest him. Instead, they would give him the harshest sentence of all: sending him home to his angry wife.

Liverpool winning in 1965 prepared me for the celebrations that were to happen in 1966. When Everton won the FA Cup Final on 14 May of that year, once again the city had cause for celebration. This time the flags were blue and the scarves were blue and white. But I didn't mind what scarf I was waving, I was happy seeing the street parties popping up again.

Like the two cathedrals, the Liverpool ground and the Everton ground weren't very far apart. And although the two teams were, and still are, arch-rivals, whenever either one had a match against an enemy team – Manchester United being top on the enemy list – the Liverpool and Everton fans would mellow and help support each other against the enemy. The Derby was a match that seemed to mellow the blue and red fans even further. This was because every single Scouse family in the city of Liverpool was made up of both Liverpool and Everton supporters. This meant they had to get along or there would be a lot of broken families and broken noses too.

The Derby made the streets of Liverpool an even more colourful place, with house windows decked out in both the red Liverpool flags and scarves, and the blue of Everton. The rivalry between two lots of supporters living in one little terraced house or flat was amazing. Dad was an Evertonian and my mam was a staunch Liverpudlian. Like Penny Page's puppet, 'Googi the Liverpool duck', sang, 'Half our house is all for red, the other half is blue. There's murder on a Saturday night when one of them get through!' Googi was a smart duck. There was always two kick-offs when the Derby came along, one on the pitch and the other surrounding the pitch. Every single one of the fans attending was a self-appointed referee, even though half of them couldn't kick a ball, never mind spell 'referee'.

Age-old rivalries between Reds and Blues were once again set aside as the city celebrated together. Nan, who at the time was a staunch Everton fan, jumped up when she heard on her radiogram that they'd won the FA Cup, and wrapped her blue and white scarf around my grandad's neck, shouting, 'We won! We won!' And – because he was probably the most dedicated Liverpool fan that has ever lived – he quickly ragged the scarf off his neck, as though laced with the black death, and nearly strangled her with it: 'Don't you put that thing round my neck!' he said with sheer disgust.

If you didn't enjoy football then Liverpool was not the place you wanted to be in the sixties. First, Liverpool FC won the FA Cup in 1965, then Everton won it in May 1966, and then in July 1966, England was through to the World Cup Final and the whole country went mad. The mascot World Cup Willie – the very first World Cup mascot ever – was a football-playing lion with England written on his top. The only lion we ever saw before that was the lion logo on the eggs you used to buy at that time.

England was set to play West Germany and Nan was so excited and patriotic, she rented a television because she, like everyone in the country, wanted to see that game, even those who didn't normally watch the footy. The television set she rented came from a shop called Telefusion in Lord Street. Me and our Brian couldn't believe our eyes when it came: 'Wow! My mam must be dead rich, either that or she's won at the bingo!' our Brian said. We always knew when Mam won at the bingo because she would give us a tanner (a sixpence) each. But she told us she hadn't won at the bingo and said the television was on the 'never-never'.

'What's the never-never, Mam?' I said.

'That means you never-never finish paying for it. So don't yous two go breaking it!'

Watching the football that day was a delight. I still wasn't a fan, but the way the two previous matches had inspired our city just filled me with the spirit of the game. Now, we were sitting in our living room about to watch the national team playing – of all countries, Germany – and in the final of the World Cup on our brand-new TV set too. This was definitely one for the books. I remember the whole family screaming and jumping out of their seats as Geoff Hurst scored the third and winning goal of his hat-trick to what became one of the most famous sayings in English football, by the BBC commentator Kenneth Wolstenholme: 'They think it's all over. It is now!'

CHAPTER THIRTEEN

FROM HERE TO THERE

When we moved house (I think I was twelve-and-a-half), we moved to a house off Chatsworth Street, which was at the top of Upper Parliament Street. I remember being in a kind of post-trauma shock at moving from the place I'd lived in all my life, but then I saw the new house and all the trauma just wisped away. It was sad seeing all our old neighbours coming out onto the balconies to wave us off, though. These had been people I had known forever and there was no way I was going to see their faces again, not unless Mam visited and dragged me along with her. Even the kids who were my mates, the neighbours' kids, would most probably become strangers, although at the time we convinced ourselves that things would stay the same between us.

People back then moved house either by carrying their belongings or pushing an old-fashioned pram laden with most of the house contents piled on top. There was no such thing as a moving van for us. You'd have to be well flippin' posh if you were hiring a removal van because there were hardly any around at the time and getting one to move your furniture would cost more than what you'd get if you sold the bleedin' lot. Every family had a moving-things-around-pram; even if they'd never had kids, they still had a pram. And any piece of furniture too large to carry – and not worth the time of day – your mam would get a voucher for Sterlers to go and get a cheap, but brand-new one.

I moved into the house with my mam and dad as, sadly, Nan had passed on by then. That was around 1969. I remember how excited we were, digging out our big pram. We loaded it with so many bits of furniture and whatnots that I was amazed the wheels managed to keep their shape, with all of us bracing for impact as we wheeled the pram off one kerb and then heaving together as we lifted it on to another. And then, there it was: 9 Baslow Walk, all brand new and shiny, like a wonderful dream. Most of the streets around that area were owned by the Catholic Church and when they were putting up the new houses, all of the Proddies said, 'I'll bet the Catholics will get all of them houses.' They weren't far wrong as we were a Catholic family and so were most of our new neighbours. I remember a neighbour called Mrs Prendergast saying to my mam that the Catholics wouldn't allow Protestant families to move into Overbury Street.

'What religion are you?' said Mam.

'Church of England.'

'Where do you live?'

'Overbury Street.'

My mam frowned and said, 'You need to get your head tested.'

We never ever had a carpet when we lived in that house because my dad couldn't afford one. When we first walked in, Dad was made up because in the hallway there were these tiles called Marley tiles that you heated up with a blower and then cut them to shape. 'We won't need a carpet in here, Margie,' he said with a large smile on his face, 'we've got Marley tiles!'

Having no carpet was never a problem in Baslow Walk, what with the Marley tiles and the new central heating that we had for the very first time. A square air vent that blew out hot air, it was fantastic and seemed like the warmest thing in the world to us who were used to being cold and huddling around dying fire embers. Although, in truth, we only used the central heating up to the day my dad saw our first heating bill – after that, we froze. Everyone ended up with a bad chest because we weren't allowed to use that central heating but, eventually, we got an electric fire. I remember Mam once said to my brother, 'Light's a ciggy,' and Brian got the silver paper from a No.6 ciggy box and tried to light it on the electric bars of the fire. Boom! He blew across the kitchen like a *Carry On* character, hair sticking up and everything.

I remember the massive garden in that house. It was probably a regular-sized garden to everyone else, but I remember boasting to a friend how big the garden was and them being confused that they couldn't see a garden that compared with Sefton Park in size. But every garden is huge when you have lots of grass and no lawn mower. We used to spot the neighbours looking across and going, 'Ooh, look at their grass! It's like *The Jungle Book* in there,' and Dad would say, 'Well, lend us your lawn mower if it's bothering ya that much!'

The neighbours were great at first, but then the council gave everyone their own bit of fencing at the front and they became territorial. It was like they thought they were royal or something, like my Prinny Charles picture all over again.

We built up a lot of happy memories in that house in Baslow Walk and I lived there until 1976, when I upped and moved to my own flat in Smithdown Lane. At first I was sad I'd moved and was convinced I'd made a mistake, but after a few nights of feeling homesick and being a pathetic bint I went out with me mates, got pissed, and was relieved there was no one waiting up and moaning at me for dragging my arse in at three o'clock in the morning.

CHAPTER FOURTEEN

THE GRANDEST NATIONAL

Along with school and football, I'd never showed an interest in horse racing when I was a kid. Well, you don't really, do you? Don't get me wrong, I loved horses. I remember wishing I had a horse whenever I watched *National Velvet* with Liz Taylor, because she looked gorgeous, riding across those summer meadows featured in the film. Nowadays, if you wished for a horse, you might actually end up getting one but, back then, no chance.

As much as I loved horses, I could never see the appeal in watching them race – it was definitely a 'man thing' to do. I remember my dad going down to the bookies every Saturday and coming back later that day with either a face like thunder or a smile you couldn't wipe off with carbolic soap. Then there were those few days of the year when Dad would have the strangest mood swings. This was Grand National season, something I really didn't give a flying fuck about, because I was out playing and having a laugh. If the Grand National had been made up of Chopper bikes or go-karts, me and me mates would have been interested as we might have been competing in it. We were go-kart and Chopper gods, but I'll get back to that subject later...

Anyway, the first time I started taking the slightest bit of interest in the Grand National was when I was ten and saw a group of women and men, all looking very smart, walking through the tenements. The men had lovely suits and ties and the women wore beautiful summer dresses. I remember thinking at the time that they must be someone famous or something like that, but the more I stared to see if I recognised them off the TV, the more I realised they were just local people heading off to a wedding or the like. It was a woman who worked in a shop nearby that I overheard say, 'Fur coats and no knickers, that lot! Off to the Grand National dressed up like they own a fuckin' horse!' I went home and asked my dad what it was all about, this Grand National thing, and he let me pick a horse. We all got to pick one, in fact. I'd get a scrap of paper and a pen, close my eyes and then stick one of our David's nappy pins down. Wherever it landed, that was the horse I was stuck with, for better or worse. Then you'd put a tanner (sixpence) on the horse you picked, even if it was at twenty thousand to one.

I don't know whether we ever won any money back off our bets, but it didn't really matter because my dad loved the sport of betting on the horses more than the money he'd win back. Although, saying that, he was a bit of a bad loser. Whenever his horse got beat, he'd point at the one that won and say, 'I was gonna pick that one, but I changed my mind at the last minute!' He was dead funny, my dad, when it came to horses. I remember once me and our Brian were moaning that we wanted to go out and and play. Dad said, 'Shurrup! Yer mam said you're not going out, so you're not going out!' So, because we were sitting with grumpy faces all twisted up, he told us to get out of the room. As I was going, I said, 'I hope your horse falls over!' And yes, it fell over, and my dad battered us and called us little witches for jinxing him. From that day on, whenever he was watching the races, he made sure we went out, no matter what Mam said.

Dad's all-time favourite horse was Red Rum, a thorough-bred steeplechaser that still holds an unbeaten record of three times Grand National winner, winning in 1973, 1974 and 1977. My dad loved a sure-fire winner – even if it meant the winnings were meagre, he would still be happy knowing that he stood a very good chance of winning. The Grand National was a dangerous race for horses and many of them got hurt during the race and would have to be put down, but Red Rum never once fell or stumbled and that made my dad his biggest fan.

CHAPTER FIFTEEN

VACCINATIONS AND THE DREADED NITTY NORA

Growing up in Liverpool meant that you would have to be on your deathbed before you got to see a proper doctor, so every family had their own self-appointed medicine man or woman. We had two in our family, Nan and Mam. They were both highly skilled in the knowledge of very cheap ancient Scouse remedies and old wives' tales. I swear if they'd have lived five hundred years previous, they would have been drowned as witches for all the concoctions they'd mix together whenever one of us got ill.

In our house remedies and cures consisted of whatever brews or ointments my mam and Nan could lay their hands on. Most of these cures – and I use that word lightly – were not passed down from mother to daughter, like you might get in an ancient tribe, but from nosy neighbour to a neighbour they'd heard had someone ill in the family. There were no hot lemon powder drinks back then, just your mam or nan's imagination and dodgily-sourced knowledge. For instance, whenever Mam heard that someone in the family had chicken pox, she'd say, 'Jackie's got chicken pox, get the kids round to hers, now!' and all of us kids who were healthy and pox-free would be shunted around to Jackie's and locked up with her poxy kids so we could all catch the chicken pox at the same time and get the inevitable over with all at once. We'd be sitting there a few days later covered in calamine lotion, scratching like fuck, with Mam saying, 'Stop scratching, you'll scar yourselves!' We'd all be sat there in disbelief, going, 'You were the one who made us get the bleedin' chicken pox in the first place!'

Then there was the vaccination bus that used to come round to the school. We all had to line up at the bus and, one by one, step inside where you would be checked for TB. They would also give you a sugar lump with some kind of concoction poured onto it that was for polio. Other times, the bus would treat you for rubella (German measles). When you queued up this time, your bottle would be going because the kids that went in before you would be leaving the bus crying their eyes out, having been attacked by some woman doctor with a mad-looking needle – a needle that left five or six puncture holes in your arm.

Then there was Nitty Nora, the nit (or biddy) doctor, who used to come to your school in a white coat and search through the pupils' hair for head louse, like she was some kind of baboon. We used to dread seeing the line waiting to go in to see Nitty Nora. The worst thing was that any one of you could have nits – you only had to be within reach of a nit-headed friend and you'd suddenly have them too. But that didn't mean you were a 'mef' or a tramp, it meant you had head lice, that's all. And everyone's bottle would go when the teacher received the paper with the running order for when your class had to go see Nora. Oh, and by the way, Nitty Nora wasn't her real name, there were lots of Noras all over the country, making kids' lives a misery. Now, I say a misery not because the kid wanted to keep his biddys, it was the pure shame you felt if it turned out that you did have nits – everyone would know. I hate to say it, but it was like the kids' equivalent of a STD test: sitting there feeling clean, with gleaming long locks and yet for all your cleanliness, you could still have a shittin' wild kingdom going on in your barnet.

Then there were the obvious cases: the kid who's as grimy as a dustman's bollocks and sat there waiting to be seen, no hope in his eyes, the results a foregone conclusion as he's already itching himself red raw. So, you both go in to see Nora and what the fuck? The plague-kid's got the all-clear and you're carrying the tell-tale 'I'm a nit-ball' letter home to your parents, where it was 'Get out the nit shampoo,' which was something you had in the cupboard, but only if you'd come into money. In my house we had to make do with Nan's vinegar, which stunk to high heaven and nearly burned your scalp off.

I remember one time me, Brian and our Ian all got a letter to take home from school. No other kids in my class got one. In fact, there were only four in the whole school who did get one and we were three of them. As I walked home with my brothers, I tried to convince each of us that we'd received the letters because we'd been really good in our classes. Good at what? I didn't have a friggin' clue, but it made us all feel a lot more positive as we stood in the lounge grinning at Mam as she opened the letters, one by one. She didn't say a word, she just took in the contents of each letter, a slight nod to herself combined with an even slighter sigh as she moved on to the next letter. Her face was a picture of study; she was obviously thinking about our reward.

'Have we been good at school, Mam?' I asked.

'Yeah,' she said.

'What have we been good at?'

'Catching.'

'Catching what?'

'Catchin' bloody nits, that's what! Now get in that friggin' bath, you dirty little buggers!'

The tin bath, normally reserved for a Sunday night's big wash, was dragged out in front of the fire and filled with scorching-hot water that was way too hot for our little bodies. Mam scrubbed us like she was cleaning the step, then Dad rubbed us down with a towel that was rougher than sandpaper as we stood on a copy of the *Liverpool Echo* to catch the drips and nits.

Nan was the next stop on the nit-destroying assembly line. She stood ready with a bottle of vinegar in one hand and a nit comb in the other. She doused our heads with vinegar and then dragged the nit comb through our hair, taking half of our scalp with it. Nan said the vinegar would burst the eggs. When the torture was over, we were all stood bawling in pain after having a worn-out nit comb rake the skin from our scalps, but we found some comfort when the nit patrol gave us a big doorstep jam butty each, although Mam added, 'That'll teach you not to hang around that nitty-headed, this name or that name!' She always had a nit-carrier friend in mind.

And so the treatment was over and, two to three weeks later, the kids in school stopped treating you like you were a leper, all was right in the world again and you immediately started hanging around with that good old nitty friend your mam hated. My mam also hated The Beatles at those times because they started the moptop hairstyle and lots of kids grew their hair longer to copy their idols, and so there became a nit epidemic. And when the hippies came along, Mam really lost her nut!

CHAPTER SIXTEEN

SCOUSE HOLIDAYS, SCHOOL TRIPS AND DAYS OUT

We never really had holidays when we were kids, we either went over to New Brighton, where there was a fairground, or to Wales, but mostly we'd have a day out in the park feeding the ducks. The only time we ever went away properly was to Talacre in North Wales when my dad had his Morris Minor (he'd bought the car with part of a compensation payout he was awarded after being in a road accident)and we would stay in someone who knew someone who knew someone with a caravan's caravan, if that makes sense. Although we could only ever stay for one night because the someone who knew someone had already rented the caravan out.

The first time we went on a proper holiday was to Butlins. We didn't have suitcases because we couldn't afford to pay for a holiday and buy new cases as well. I remember as we were walking in with our holiday gear in plastic carrier bags, this woman asked in a friendly way, 'Have you been to the launderette? Could you tell me where it is?' and we just cringed with shame because she had clearly thought our plastic holiday bags were for carrying our laundry. She must have been near-sighted because since when have washing bags had 'Tesco' written on them? I think it was the only time I've ever had matching luggage!

Uncle Freddie's van was exactly like a second-hand police black Mariah, or 'meat wagon', as we used to call them. We would go on trips for the day out in the van and half the family used to pile into the back. There was our Sandra and Billy, with their kids, Lisa and Colin. Then there was Aunty Mary and Uncle Freddy, with their kids, Jackie and Alan. Also, our Jean and Joey, with Stephen and Andrew. My mam and dad, me, Ian and David too. Honestly, we looked like a pissing motley crew getting off to rob a bank! We'd have no seat belts or nothing to hold onto when the van turned corners, so by the time we got to where we were going, we'd all be battered and shaken up.

Mam used to stick the Primus stove in the back with us, which would usually end up on top of us. Sometimes we would go to a campsite in Wales or Blackpool. We would all pile out and Mam would light up the stove and start cooking burgers and sausages and the like. There were so many of us queuing up for burgers and the line was so long, on more than one occasion people who weren't in the family started queuing up also, because they thought it was a paid burger van.

We'd play Rounders on the beach until one of us started

moaning about his or her turn, then my dad would say, 'That's it now!' and we'd have to go back to the van, all of us poking and prodding the one little moaner who spoilt the fun for everyone else. After we'd been on the campsite for a couple of days, Dad would wait until the middle of the night and he and our Freddy would wake us all up so we could do a bunk without paying. Watching us trying to get dressed and tripping over each other in the dark was like something from a Monty Python film, honestly.

My school trips I remember with mixed emotions. Climbing on to a coach that looked as though the last time it heard the word 'MOT' was in 1910. Strangely enough, at the time us kids had no fear whatsoever as we clambered aboard, clutching bottles of sherbet water and jam or sugar butties, or for those with well-off parents, banana butties. Sometimes you used to get those kids who'd bug you for your sandwiches, always cadging and never bringing any of their own, either because their parents couldn't afford the snacks or they were just greedy bastards who'd eaten theirs and now wanted to eat yours too. Other times, you'd get the bullies threatening to kick your face in if you didn't give them half – if not all – of your sandwiches.

There was a brief spell when I got to take meat paste sandwiches on neighbourhood and school trips, and when the cadgers and bullies used to come after my sandwiches, they would end up with a specially prepared sandwich made with cat food that smelled exactly like the salmon from the paste jars. Once the cadgers and bullies tasted the cat food sandwiches that they thought were salmon paste, they never bothered me again.

We never went far on the coaches, maybe to Calderstones Park. Once there, we would pick up conkers and leaves. We'd make rubbings of any signs with paper and crayons and then we'd take them back to school to show all the naughty kids that exactly what they'd missed out on.

One time we went canoeing with Paddy Comp – which was my school at the time – to Greenbank Park at the bottom of Ullet and Smithdown Road. The park had a lovely lake, where all of the students from Greenbank College were chilling and sat round listening to music. We weren't allowed to chill as we were with a particularly prick-like teacher who wanted us to go out on the lake in canoes. Before then we had never even sat in a canoe, but that didn't occur to Mr Shite-for-brains teacher as he started raising his voice until we eventually pushed off from the lakeside.

'Now, lean to one side and roll into the water and up again!' he said. What the fuck? is what we were thinking in our little individual canoes. 'Roll now!' he shouted, and so we leaned over and rolled. Everyone else came back up, but I stayed under, nearly drowning because my friggin' canoe was broke or something. It eventually rolled up and I was nearly crying with shock. Then, as I paddled back to the lakeside, the cheeky tit of a teacher started whacking me with his paddle. 'Fuck you and your canoe!' I shouted.

That was the first day I got suspended from Paddy Comp.

Another time, we went fell walking to Blue John mines in

Buxton with, you guessed it, Paddy Comp. It was beautiful around that part of the country and inside the mine was a sight to see, absolutely stunning. All of us kids were in awe and having a great time until the dumb-arsed teacher said we had to go potholing deep into the mine. At first it was not too bad and rather like a Jules Verne adventure, then the cave got smaller and smaller until it was like trying to squeeze through a fuckin' Smarties tube. There were kids in front of me and behind me, we were in the smallest place I'd been in since the womb, and I suddenly realise I've got claustrophobia. I scream like there's no tomorrow and then the other kids in front and behind start screaming because they think there's been a cave in or something.

'I wanna get out now!' I yelled.

I was hitting my head on the bloody cave ceiling and I had the water we were crawling through spilling into my mouth, so I really did feel like I couldn't breathe. Once again, I got bollocked out by my teachers. We were in Buxton for one week and me and my friend Carla ended up in hospital, suffering from exposure. We'd been told that we had to wear pure wool socks when fell walking, but we had cheap nylon thin ones because our parents couldn't really afford wool just for use on a one-week school trip, so we ended up in Buxton hospital. Every time we tried to nod off to sleep, the doctors would smack us in the face and shout at us to stay awake – I think it was because we might have slipped into a coma or something like that. Whatever it was, we kept on swearing whenever they smacked us, but the teacher couldn't say anything because the doctor said our swearing was probably due to our condition. Needless to say, we let rip!

Colomendy in North Wales deserves a chapter all to itself, but it isn't going to get one, because everyone who went there already knows most of what went on there. So, if you were one of the fortunate (or unfortunate) Colomendy visitors then you might want to skip the next bit; either that, or read on and revel in the nostalgia. We went there with our school – St Saviour's – because it was free to go, simple as that. At the time we were receiving free school dinners so everything else that could possibly be free was free. We were so excited we were going that one silly sod of a girl actually pissed herself with excitement all over the coach seat. The tune that was No.1 in the charts at that time was Desmond Dekker, '(Poor Me) The Israelites', and it must have come on the coach radio ten times at least, with all of us kids screaming out the chorus. Good enough, the teacher in charge screamed out the chorus along with us.

I think we'd been fooled into thinking Colomendy was going to be like a holiday camp, because the only people in Wales who weren't Welsh were there on their holidays. It turned out to be a weird outdoor school, which we all hated, but going there was worth it as we got to drive through the Mersey Tunnel for the very first time – not many parents had cars back in them days. I can still remember the teacher shouting at us to put the windows up in case we got carbon monoxide poisoning. I also remember us pretending that the tunnel had sprung a leak: 'Oh, sir, look, it's dripping! The

River Mersey's gonna crash down and drown us all!' The teacher would be having a fit, running along the coach and shouting at us to behave because we were making the more timid classmates cry their eyes out.

The mad thing was that the coach driver didn't say anything because he'd just come from having a couple of pints in a pub and was now driving a coach full of kids while smoking away like Puffing Billy. Back then, anything was allowed: kids were encouraged to climb dangerously high things just for the exercise, and coach drivers were allowed two or more pints en route; not legally, I suppose, but none of the teachers ever seemed to pull them for drink driving. Most probably because the teachers would have had a few skinfulls along the way. We used to gauge just how much booze the coach driver had knocked back by the amount of swerving he did across the road. If you could hear the tyres screeching now and again then you knew he'd been pigging out in the pub and now he wasn't sure where the hell he was. And if he started swearing and shoving two fingers up to the traffic around him, you held on tight to something as it was gonna be a bumpy ride! We just hoped that he would stop on the way so he could breathe some air, have a couple more fags and maybe sober up a little.

On the bus, singing was a big deal. It was voluntary to join in, but everyone did. This was really weird because no one voluntarily joined in when it came to singing prayers at school assembly. But I suppose we liked these songs because they were about silly subjects that had ten people in one bed and then someone being pushed out: 'There were ten in the bed and the little one said, "Roll over, roll over," and they all rolled over and one fell out...' Well, if you ever went on a coach as a kid then you'll know the rest. We loved singing those songs and it would take ages to get through each one, which was great for kids who got travel sick as it would distract them from puking up and stinking the coach out.

When we finally got to Colomendy and I opened my bag, the teacher asked, 'Christine, where have all your clothes gone?' because I only possessed two pairs of knickers – one in the wash and one I had on – and a Liberty bodice (like a vest with rubber buttons up the front, which was meant to keep you extra warm in winter, even though you'd fall asleep on your belly and wake up looking like a flute). But it was either wear a Liberty bodice or the woollen jumpers my nan used to knit that would have you scratching to death because the wool was so coarse.

Looking around Colomendy made you wish that you hadn't bothered turning up for the coach. It looked the same as school, but in the middle of nowhere and freezing bloody cold, even though it was the middle of summer. Although it looked like school, there was one notable difference...you never got to go home at three o'clock. So, in other words, you were locked in school for days. 'Whose fuckin' bright idea was this?' I remember thinking to myself after being there for ten minutes. There were the upper and lower camps, these long huts that had all the kids sleeping in them, and you had to sleep in a bunk bed, which wasn't that bad a thing because, for some reason, bunk beds are exciting to kids. Smelling each other's farts and having to listen to someone snoring and pissing the bed all night is apparently a great thing when you're little. I was just happy that I had a bed to myself for the first time in…? Forever!

Things of note at Colomendy were the tuck shop, which was always crammed with goodies, but you had to make your money last, so we – me and my school mates – would make sure none of us blew our cash on day one. My school mates were usually different to the ones I played with after school. I suppose you could compare it to the mates you went to clubs with and the ones you went on holiday with – 'Oh, East is East, and West is West, and never the twain shall meet…'

There were always the kids who had lots of money, who would end up buying half of the tuck shop on day one. If we were lucky, one of those minted kids would be a school friend. Sometimes you would make sure you had extra money in your pocket by selling your free school dinner tickets in advance. You would always search out the kid who looked like he or she enjoyed a meal or ten, and do the old *Godfather* trick: 'make them an offer they can't refuse'. Tickets for half the price of the school meal? SOLD! Even if the school meals were fuckin' horrendous, it didn't matter to those greedy kids who would eat so fast the food never hit their taste buds.

There were lots of fights at Colomendy, usually with another school's students, who were staying in the other long hut. Never in any other situation as a kid would you be required to instantly hate a bunch of strangers, every last one of them. Although you might spot one or two lads you liked and meet up with them later behind the dorms. Not me though, remember I was the funny one, not the 'eyes meet across the Colomendy court yard' one. Even if some lad did have his eye on me, I probably wouldn't have noticed. Most of the time I'd be too engrossed in eating one of those liquorice sticks that dipped into sherbet. So, I always had black lips with bits of sherbet sprinkled on them – very attractive to the opposite sex...not!

I remember sitting on my bunk bed, the top one, and looking down at the criers – the kids who wished they hadn't come because they missed their mams and dads. I missed mine, and especially my Nan, but I wasn't going to whinge about it as I was preparing myself for being freaked out that night by someone pretending to be Pegleg Pete, the pirate ghost of Colomendy. We'd heard in advance that on your first night at Colomendy, some tit would always start making ghost noises that would have everyone in the dorm kicking off. They would moan along the dorm, pretending to be the legendary pirate Pegleg Pete, who apparently came to an unfortunate end at...Colomendy? Well, we all know a ghost story doesn't have to make the slightest bit of sense to scare the shite out of you – I mean, have a listen to my mam's stories. Anyway, we all spent the first night wide awake and freaked out, so the next day, when we went to scale the mountain called Moel Famau, we all gave up within minutes of starting our ascent because of a serious lack of sleep.

One of the creepiest memories I have about my so-called

holiday in Colomendy was seeing my two female teachers – Miss Bradshaw and Miss Lace – walking around the dorms in their nighties. I don't know why it was so creepy but it definitely disturbed me a bit, seeing my teachers in their night-gear – ugh! Almost everything at Colomendy bugged me: the showers were horrible, full of damp and cold as fuck. The lads would always kick footballs at you whenever you passed the footy field. The catwalk in Devil's Gorge made you crap yourself, thinking you were about to plummet to your death, and the school disco was just stupid, but hilarious, as kids of that age can't dance. All in all, Colomendy was a beautiful disaster, a childhood one-off experience not to be missed.

CHAPTER SEVENTEEN

RELIGION...FOR CHRIST'S SAKE!

O ne of the most famous buildings in Liverpool stands at the bottom of Renshaw Street in the city centre. St Luke's Church, now known as 'The Bombed-out Church', took a direct hit from a German bomb during the Blitz. All those inside the church who were praying for peace were killed instantly. The church was gutted, but still stands as a reminder of what Liverpool City endured.

As well as having two famous football teams, Liverpool also has two famous cathedrals that stand on opposite ends of the same street. Hope Street stretches from the Catholic Cathedral (Metropolitan Cathedral or 'Paddy's Wigwam' as we always called it) on Mount Pleasant, right the way along to the gothic splendour of the Anglican Cathedral (Dracula's Castle) at Upper Parliament Street. The construction of the Metropolitan Cathedral started in 1962. While the Anglican Cathedral, or 'Proddy Cathedral' as my mam, dad and nan used to call it, was started in 1904 and only completed in 1978, which meant the fellas who started building it were probably buried somewhere near it by the time it was finished.

Being Catholic or Protestant was one of Liverpool's touchiest subjects. Windsor Hall Sunday School – where I used to go now and then – didn't care if you were Catholic or Protestant as long as you filled their numbers and agreed to listen to all things Jesus-like. Any other church would care what denomination you were. Catholic and Protestant, the two hated each other and they still do. I couldn't think of a subject that arose when I was a kid that would cause more spitting and clenching of teeth. It was like a silent war going on in Liverpool, two lots of people forced to live side by side, but just waiting for any kind of kick-off to vent their spleen. Catholics disliked Protestants, Protestants didn't seem to give a shit and just went about their business.

The Orange Lodge, however, were Protestants that fuckin' loathed Catholics. When I was growing up, each year on 12 July, the Orange Lodge – who were seen by Catholics as extreme Protestants – would converge on Exchange Street train station, where the steam trains would carry all of the different Lodges into Southport, and me and me mate Maureen Gee would go to watch them setting off. When we went home later, smelling of smoke from the trains, I'd get a clip round the ear from Nan, saying, 'You've been down there watching those Proddy dogs again, haven't you?' and I'd be like, 'No, Nan, no, I haven't!' But I couldn't help following them to the station because where else were you going to see twenty or more marching bands, all playing Irish music as they marched to the beat of a drum? I was a kid, for God's sake, and marching bands were friggin' amazing to me, no matter what their religious affiliation.

We used to stand on Parliament Street when the bands marched by to see if anyone was insane enough to attempt crossing the road and – as the Lodge members called it – 'breaking their ranks'. This was only ever attempted by one of the more crazy, head-the-ball, all-out nutcases you could find, who didn't really give a shit what the Lodge thought and was going to cross the ranks and get to the betting office early, band or no friggin' band. Most of the Lodge band members were usually spoiling for a fight anyway, so this was the perfect impetus for an all-out kick-off. Suddenly, the instruments that up to a moment ago had been making great music were now bouncing off someone's head, because that self-same Catholic guy who broke the Orange ranks always had a back-up of onlookers, who were also Catholic and ready to dive in to protect their God's chosen.

Back then, both sides started the fights, taking turns as to which one would actually start the ball rolling, but I must admit that the Lodge did tend to march into areas where they knew there'd be a kick-off, like the Bullring tenements as they knew the Bullring was a staunch Catholic area, as was most of Liverpool 8. It was a bit of a pain for people who had both Catholics and Protestants in the same family as they were always at each other's throats.

Anyone who's ever been to see the Anglican cathedral – or

the 'Proddy Cathedral' as us Catholics called it – will know that it looks like some kind of gothic building from the realms of either *Dracula*, *Frankenstein* or even King Arthur. The fifth largest cathedral in the world, it was designed by Sir Giles Gilbert Scott – the same man who designed Battersea Power Station and those red telephone boxes you see less and less of nowadays. He was the grandson of George Gilbert Scott, the guy who designed all the workhouses – have you read *Oliver Twist*, or, like me, seen the musical where asks for more gruel? Yes, well, that building was a workhouse. Well done, Mr George Gilbert friggin' Scott! Your name will be synonymous with misery for centuries to come.

Anyway, at the base of the cathedral lie the cathedral grounds, or St James's Cemetery, a huge graveyard with slopes to walk up, tombs to have a nose in, and lots and lots of gravestones. The gravestones have names on them that sound like they've come straight out of a Dickens' novel, which – if you'll allow me to digress for a moment, is a very interesting thing. You see, Charles Dickens himself once gave readings at the school opposite the Anglican cathedral, The Liverpool Institute. And in the cathedral grounds there is one gravestone that has a list of the children who died in Liverpool's workhouses – stay with me, I do have a friggin' point to all this! So, one of the names on the gravestone is Oliver, and further down on the same gravestone is the name Twist. Now, I reckon Charlie Dickens, while on his lunch break, took a stroll down to the cathedral graveyard to eat his sandwiches, saw the gravestone with both Oliver and Twist carved on it, and the rest is history. No? Well, I think it's a bit of a coincidence. Whatever, suit yourselves, and excuse me for thinking you might have found it interesting. Anyway – digressing over – to me and me mates the cathedral graveyard was like a Scouse Disneyland. The whole thing was dug out of a quarry, which they say the sandstone from the quarry went to build half of the expensive houses in the area. The slopes, or paths of the graveyard, zigzagged up to street level and had tombs dug into the walls running alongside the slopes. Most of these tombs had been wrecked ages ago and some had been broken into, so we would dare each other to see which one of us was brave enough to enter the tomb alone. Once one of us did go in, the rest would block the entrance and start screaming that there was something coming to get them in the dark. This activity would always turn into a full-on fight as there was always one of your mates who took the joke too far and tried sealing you in the tomb with nettle bushes or anything else they could lay their hands on.

Another thing we loved in the 'Gravey' – our nickname for the graveyard – was climbing the German wall. I'm not sure why it was called the German wall, but it was massive and the largest of the walls that surrounded the graveyard. The wall wasn't completely vertical, and you could – if you were mad enough – attempt to slide down it. Me and me mates were a bit crazy so we often tried sliding down, starting cautiously slow and hitting breakneck speed within seconds. Luckily, there was a soft landing of grass and very bouncy soil to break your fall.

Most of the walls, including part of the German wall, had gaps where the mortar had crumbled between the sandstone blocks. This made it really easy to scale the walls. I can imagine what we must have looked like to anyone walking through the grounds, a bunch of girls clinging to the wall at different heights, all very unladylike and laughing our heads off because one of us had told a joke, usually me. There was one time when Jeanie, my bezzy mate at the time, climbed along a part of the wall that had a tree growing out of it and disturbed a wasps' nest that seemed to be wrapped around one of its branches. All of us had to risk life and limb to jump off the wall from whatever height we were at.

The wasps were brutal and chased us right across the Gravey. The only way we got rid was by running into a group of uniformed school boys and then running off in the opposite direction. The wasps immediately turned their focus towards the boys, poor buggers. I know my mates didn't feel guilty, in fact they were laughing for the most part, but I felt bad for getting those boys stung by the wasps.

I loved hanging out in that graveyard because there were so many things to occupy your mind. And unlike most things, the Liverpool parks being the other exception, you didn't have to fork out any money to have a day of fun and sheer delight.

Other things we liked doing down in the Gravey included screaming our heads off through the bars of William Huskisson's tomb. British statesman, financier and MP Huskisson was the first unfortunate guy to be run over by a train in Britain. Now, remember, this was when trains went around two miles an hour, top speed! So, I have no notion as to how the train managed to catch up with Huskisson to run him over, poor bugger.

As you screamed into the tomb or made whatever ridiculous grunting sounds or fart noises, your voice would echo and could be heard all over the graveyard. Huskisson's tomb stood in front of a wall of bare brick and sandstone that had a small trickle of water pouring from a copper pipe sticking out from the wall. The trickle was, and is, Liverpool's natural spring, discovered in the eighteenth century. It was supposed to give you vitality and make you spring about, which – if you'd have seen the lot of us prancing about and scaling walls like ants on the side of a picnic table after having a drink of it – you'd have believed every bloody word!

To the right of the tomb stood a single grave at the fork of two paths. We liked this grave because once on a visit to the graveyard with my mam, she told me that it was the grave of Kitty Wilkinson, known as 'Saint of the Slums', who made the first washhouses for the poor and the first combined washhouses and public baths. When Mam told me that, I wondered if I would ever do anything as good as Kitty had done with her washhouses that went on to save people from a cholera epidemic. I suppose my achievement lies in swearing like I was in a bloody washhouse!

Another gravestone that caught my attention in the Gravey – not to be morbid or anything, droning on about pissin' gravestones the whole time – was a strange little stone that stood at the base of the German wall. It was odd because it was so close to the wall and while all the other gravestones faced away, this one stood facing the wall. The name on the gravestone was Oliver Cromwell. Now, as some of you might know – or having listened to me for more than ten seconds might have guessed – I didn't do well in school. But I do remember a lot of what we were taught and one of the names that stuck in my head as pouring from the mouth of our boring arsed history teacher was Oliver Cromwell. And for some time I thought the cathedral Gravey was where the once Lord Protector of England was buried. Then one day I noticed that this Oliver Cromwell died aged one. I always wondered why parents would have their child's gravestone face a wall. If anyone reading this can enlighten me, please let me know (by coming to one of my stand-up shows, paying your entrance fee at the door and setting up an unlimited tab for me at the bar).

As I mentioned earlier, the graveyard contained gravestones that listed the deaths of children from the workhouses, and me and my friends – like any healthy British kids – had a morbid fascination with the dead. We'd stand there for ages reading out the names of the children listed on the workhouse and orphanage gravestones. Leach, Twist, Grigg, Wick, Bland could all have come straight from the pages of a Dickens' novel, only these poor toddlers died on average at one or two years of age. 'It must have been such a bloody horrible time, being poor in Victorian England,' we'd say, and it made us realise that we had a lot more than we appreciated.

Yep, the cathedral Gravey was definitely one of the best

playgrounds you'd want to spend your time in. You could be ragging each other's hair and trying to claw each other's eyes out for trapping you in a tomb. Next minute, you're best friends again, yelling fart noises into Huskisson's tomb, then rounding off the day as best friends singing songs together and marching up the winding path out of the Gravey, arms around each other's shoulders.

While I'm on the subject of religion, I should really mention a very nice man called Mr Coffee. Now, Mr Coffee was one of the people who first got me interested in going to church, but for all the wrong reasons. A black man, who stood about 5'3", he had the most immaculately polished shoes on, I always remember. He always wore a pristine trilby and suit. Every time he'd see you, he'd have a great big grin on his face and say, 'Hello! Have you been to see Jesus?' And he loved Jesus, did Mr Coffee. His enthusiasm made us all love Jesus too, because there in the middle of all the debris stood Windsor Hall church, where he used to frequent. It was a small church me and my brother Brian would play in and around. There, we used to see Aunty Edie, a little lady who wore the same old-fashioned shoes to church every Sunday. We always thought Aunty Edie smelled peculiar, but we could never work out what she smelled of. Eventually, I found out that the smell was from mothballs, used to keep the moths away from an already moth-eaten fur coat she wore to church services. Edie would say, 'Come on down the stairs and I'll tell you a story of Jesus.' And we'd say, 'No, thanks, we want to keep playing.' But as soon as she added,

'You'll get orange juice and a biscuit if you come down,' we would fly down those stairs in a shot. And for that reason we thought Jesus was fantastic because he once supplied the masses with fishes and loaves, and now he supplied us kids with orange juice and biscuits.

The Catholic Cathedral wasn't somewhere we played a lot, but we did play there sometimes on our way back from messing around in TJ Hughes department store on London Road. The crypt was a night shelter, where the homeless used to go and get soup and somewhere to sleep away from the cold. My weirdest memory of the cathedral was when all the nuns got married to the Church – lying prostrate, dressed all in white, arms out – being married to God and Jesus Christ. To me this was a little scary at the time as they all looked like they were in a trance, or maybe that was just my overactive imagination. I remember we used to like running up and down the cathedral steps until we were panting like dogs – we must have looked like a load of little Rocky Balboas!

When my nan passed away in 1969, Mam started to take us to a Spiritualist church as a way to try and keep some kind of link with her. I must have been eleven or twelve and Mam used to take me to this strange church on a Sunday. She always used to say, 'Don't you tell your dad you come here.' She knew he'd go mental if he found out. The Liverpool Spiritualist Church was, and is, situated near the Liverpool Royal hospital on Daulby Street, and the reason my dad wasn't a fan was because, like most churches, the Liverpool Spiritualist Church used to have a donation box, which my mam was happy to help fill if she thought it might keep that link open with my recently deceased Nan. The average donation was ten bob (50 pence in today's money), but my mam used to give a lot more than that. I can still see Dad flying off the handle because he'd spot us sneaking back in the house after a long church visit, and he'd know that the Church now had more of our money than we did.

'Don't be going down there, giving them bastards our money!' he'd say. 'The only friggin' spirit they see is in the pub on the corner and his name's Johnnie Walker!'

Dad always made out that the people running the place were all drunks who – after every Sunday service – would take the donations to the corner pub and get pissed as hell. The way he'd describe their so-called underhanded goings-on, you'd swear he had photographic evidence. Like he'd been sitting in one of those unmarked vans you see in American cop movies, loaded with surveillance equipment.

'They're having you off, Margie!' he'd shout till he was blue in the face. 'There's no such thing as ghosts, and if there were, they wouldn't turn up to see that bunch of dickheads! Do you really think your ma would want you giving your money to them lot of rip-offs?'

Mam would just roll her eyes and say, 'Oh go on with you, it's only ten bob!'

'Ten bob? I'll tell ya fuckin' fortune for ten bob!'

He mostly said it tongue-in-cheek, though – I think his aim was to just wind her up. Ooh, he used to love tormenting the life out of my mam when it came to that spiritualist church.

He used to go, 'Here, Margie, I've got a message for ya. Y'know when you go the bingo on Thursday, well, wooooo! You're not going!'

In all honesty, the organisers of the Sunday ghost show, as I used to call it, never once took the donations down to their local pub; they believed in what they were saying one hundred per cent and any donations went straight back into the Church to fund more colourful Sunday readings.

I was fascinated with it all. I'd done the Catholic Sunday school – 'lament or die in a river of fire, with a pitchfork up your arse' kind of thing – for too many years, now here was something akin to *The Jerry Springer Show*, but with disembodied spirits. I'll never forget one Sunday, the guy in charge – I'm not sure if he was called a priest, father, or something like that – stood up in front of the crowd – who really weren't that arsed about anything but hearing from their own deceased relatives – and he started talking about dead pets. There was a cat called Sailor floating around and circling his feet, but nobody knew whose ghost cat it was, although some old biddy with a giant hearing aid said she once knew a Korean sailor. The spiritualist ringmaster continued by saying he had the spirit of a dog called Mandy... Nope! No reaction from the crowd whatsoever. Lastly, he said something was flying around his head and landing on his shoulder: 'It's a budgie, and it's happy to be free of its cage, although it really does miss its family. The budgie's name is Joey!' Oh, the whole fuckin' place went nuts! Turns out at the time half of Liverpool once owned a budgie called Joey.

I don't think Mam ever received a message from my nan on any of those Sundays we visited that church, but it did give her, and a lot of the Joey-the-budgie lovers a sense of hope that they didn't always get from the Catholic Church, with its damnation of all things even the slightest bit enjoyable. Hope that one day they would be reunited with loved ones passed, and there might be a chance that they would get to talk to them again before that day. For that reason, no matter how much Dad griped or ripped the piss out of my poor mother, the weekly ten-bob donation was well worth it.

The year 1969, was the year the lunar space module *Eagle* landed on the moon and, for a lot of people, this event signals the end of Christianity. We'll get back to the religious bit in a minute because I want to talk about Michael Collins. Yeah, the guy that isn't Neil Armstrong – owner of the first foot on the moon – or Buzz Aldrin, the guy who got to be a toy in the film *Toy Story*. No, I'm talking about the guy who travelled the 384,400 kilometres to the moon and didn't get to touch the fucker: no claim, no fame. Even Yuri Gagarin – who only went into space – was far more famous than Michael Collins, and Gagarin was only a few miles closer to the moon than the rest of us. How pissed off would you be, all the way up there and you're told to stay on the spaceship and keep the engine running? Ooh, he must have hated that, as his only claim to fame was being the guy who 'never' walked on the moon! I'm sure that his job was just as important as the two big-headed lucky bastards who did get to do a moonwalk, but to be honest, as a kid I didn't even know there was a third guy. I do remember being stupidly excited though, because landing on the moon was such a big deal for the whole of humanity. Not just the Americans, who actually got there, but for the rest of us who now knew that most probably anything was possible.

The men landing on the moon did kill Christianity, though. Before men went into space, everybody thought that heaven was just above the clouds. Then all of a sudden the clouds with angels leading the way up to heaven didn't exist because man had gone beyond the clouds and there were no pearly gates or harps, or anything else, just the vacuum of space. So, where was God? That's how I looked at it. And whenever we went to church after that, I was a lot more doubtful as to what was being preached to us because it didn't fit with the fact that man had been to the moon and back and saw nothing in between.

I also used to worry myself by thinking, if there's nothing out there but space, where do you go when you die? When Nan died, I was looking for her, and thought she couldn't come home because the last thing she ever said to me was, 'I never brought me glasses.' So, I thought she'd gone and couldn't get home because she couldn't see the way without her glasses on. I used to go out looking for her with her glasses in my hand. And I remember being so mentally exhausted, unable to find her, that I'd sit on the doorstep, crying. Aunty Edie – the lady from the church – once said to me, 'Your Nan's gone to heaven, girl.' And I remember asking, 'How has she gone to heaven? How did she get there if she couldn't see the way without glasses?' Aunty Edie just smiled and said, 'Have you ever fallen asleep on the chair or the floor, but you wake up in bed and you wonder how you got there?' I nodded. 'Well, that's the wonder of Jesus. And when you fall asleep and you die, then Jesus comes and he picks you up, and when you awake, you're in heaven, so there's no need for you to see the way.'

I remember thinking I have to go to heaven because if Nan's there, I can give her the glasses, then she can see her way back to us and Mam won't be sad and crying any more. But when the men walked on the moon, I started questioning where was God? Even worse, was my nan on the moon? I didn't like those thoughts because you're supposed to have blind faith in God and Jesus, whether things make sense or not. I remember asking my friend, 'Where's Heaven then? The spacemen never saw it, so where the Hell is it?' My friend, who was always a bit of a smart arse, just said, 'It's where it's always been, just left of where the men in the rocket were flying. In fact, they just clipped Heaven when they flew past.' I think what she was trying to tell me was that space is massive, so unless the guys in the rocket were aiming for it, they would have missed it by miles.

Another, more hippyish, friend said that the reason the astronauts never saw heaven was because it's always daylight in heaven and where the astronauts went was dark. So, at that time, heaven was on the other side of the earth's clouds in the daylight.

Fuck, did I have some dickhead mates when I was a kid!

CHAPTER EIGHTEEN

MINISKIRTS, HIPPIES AND GLAM

I was seven in 1965, our Brian was five, and The Beatles were the biggest band in history. All of the older generation – including my nan – were moaning and spitting their false teeth out because they found The Beatles shocking and a bad influence on the youth of the day, with their long hair and their Tickets to Ride. 'Ride? Ride bleedin' where?' Nan used to say, red-faced. 'I wish they'd flippin' ride! Ride off, so I wouldn't have to listen to their caterwauling anymore!'

The skirts got shorter in sixty-five, with the introduction of the miniskirt, and the hair got a lot longer. The skirts were another thing Nan would vent her spleen over. She'd say, 'God almighty, look at the state of that! It looks more like a belt than a skirt, and it's high up enough to keep the rain off her head. She'll catch her bleedin' death in that. It can't be good for her kidneys!'

My nan seemed to be obsessed with kidneys, oh, and haemorrhoids too.

Many of the times sitting on the front doorstep you'd get a clip round your lugs – 'Get up off the step or you'll get piles!' Then it would be 'Always keep your back warm or you'll get bad kidneys,' hence the Liberty bodice we were always told to put on.

I remember hot pants also topped Nan's list of clothing that would destroy your kidneys. My first pair started out as a pair of red trousers with elastic around the waist. They were like bell bottoms and I hated them because everyone else was wearing hot pants and I couldn't get a pair. So, I cut the legs off the red trousers, fashioned a bib, and although everybody else thought they looked like crap, I thought they looked lovely and were the perfect accompaniment to the plazzy choker that I wore at the time. Now, this choker, my pride and joy, was my most fave thing to wear. If I'd have made a will at the time it would have insisted that I be buried with the choker round my neck. Made from finest plastic, it had a cheap cameo stuck to the front of it. My dad used to lose his rag whenever he saw me wearing that choker: 'Get that bleedin' thing off! Only prostitutes wear chokers!' Then he'd add, 'And only cats and whores stay out till the time you do!' So, me and me mates would make cat wailing sounds just to wind him up.

Hippies always stand out in my memories because – not meaning to get my stereotyping knickers on – they were the first people I ever saw smoking weed, pot…marijuana, baby!

They seemed to be saying, 'Fuck the oppressive system, we're going to chill and get stoned!' At least that's the message me and my friends seemed to get from them. One minute you'd see a bearded hippie standing in front of a crowd, saying that the world is only concerned with deodorants and how their hair is conditioned; that he and his hippie friends weren't concerned with the West's obsession with cleanliness. The next, the same guy would be lying on the park grass, smoking grass while some hippie chick would be rubbing oils into his hair and braiding it with daisies.

I remember there were so many of them lying on the grass in Princes Park, it looked like a smaller version of Woodstock. Their brightly coloured clothes almost gave me a headache. The music was loud, but hypnotising – I suppose they wanted to be hypnotised to go along with the copious amount of weed they were all smoking. For people who wanted to change the world, they spent an awful lot of time off-planet! I liked them because they were very kid-friendly. For instance, if you spoke to a hippie, they would always take the time to talk back to you. And they were super-mellow too. I once sat on the grass with a group in Sefton Park because me mate Lin wanted to see if they'd give her some weed so she could sell it to some dickhead guy she was trying to impress. But when she asked them if they had any, they just pretended they didn't know what she was talking about. I think they might have thought she was a midget policewoman in disguise as she had a very 'bizzie woman' look about her. It was her hairstyle, I think – it looked like the kind of barnet a history teacher would have, perhaps because her parents were Jehovah's Witnesses.

But I wasn't bothered about weed – I just asked the hippies about the clothes they were wearing, why they liked paisley and putting braids and flowers in their kids' hair. This one hippie lady with shining bright sea-green eyes braided my scruffy hair – what there was of it – into three smart braids. And I was sooo chuffed because two boys looked at me that day and smiled. So, I tried keeping my hair like that, but no one I knew would braid it for me.

I once saw hippies dancing in the street in the middle of Smithdown Road, like they couldn't see the traffic or something, and my mate Lin wanted to go over and ask for weed as she thought they must definitely have some because they were dancing with the traffic. I told her not to bother as they were only stopping traffic in protest of something or other, although I really wanted to go over and ask if any of them was any good at braiding hair.

March 1971, I was watching *Top of the Pops* on telly when suddenly my legs went all weak at the knees: Marc Bolan and his group T Rex were singing a song called 'Hot Love'. I had never heard of T Rex or Marc Bolan, but I loved the way he looked. He had shimmering clothes and glitter on his face and I was in love with the whole look. Soon after, glitter and glam took over the music scene with David Bowie's Ziggy Stardust, Slade, and I hate to mention the perv's name, Gary Glitter an' all. My favourite was Marc Bolan and by the time he sang 'Get It On', I was well and truly hooked.

Glitter sales must have gone through the roof back then as everyone I knew was wearing glitter on their faces and sequins on their clothes. I wore glitter tears just like Marc Bolan, and I always used to moan at my friends – who I roped in to help me achieve the look – to try and get both lots of tears matching. At that time my whole gang of friends, guys included, was walking round looking like they were dressed in multi-coloured tin foil! I know Mam thought we were dressed like that because of the moon landing, some years before.

When Marc Bolan got his own TV show – *Marc* – we watched it religiously. We never missed one show, and we all kept a small photograph in our bags that was covered, for protection, with sticky-back plastic. My friends and I had moved on from following Marc and T Rex by 1977, but we still liked their music, and so we were really shocked and saddened when he died in an accident that year. I saw Marc's funeral on the news. It was attended by lots of big names from the music industry, including glam-rock giants David Bowie and Rod Stewart amongst others. RIP for ever, Marc.

The early to mid-seventies saw some of the most ridiculous clothing trends and I loved them all! Marc Bolan, then Abba, and then The Bay City Rollers all loved wearing flared trousers and my wardrobe was full of them. Flares were great – even James Bond (Roger Moore) was wearing flares, though I could never figure out why a guy who's always running around fighting and climbing stuff would opt for wearing trousers that get snagged on everything snag-able, and leather-soled shoes that could slip on sandpaper. Flares were cool, but over-flared trousers were just the biggest fashion fuck-up ever. Birmingham bags – or 'Birmo's' as they were called by us teenagers – were the worst. High waistbands so high they could chafe your eyebrows, legs so wide you could hide four mates behind them, and some Birmo's had turn-ups at the bottom that you could lose your shopping in!

I remember getting the latest platform shoes that were so high they should have come with a vertigo warning. They were red and yellow and cost an absolute packet, and yet nobody knew I had them because the Birmo's completely covered them. What the fuck were the designers thinking? If you tried to climb over railings, you would end up snagging yourself and headbutting the railings upside down, and when walking, you stood the chance of catching your foot in the opposite trouser leg and smashing your face on the pavement. The Birmingham bags also had an added extra just to mess you up that one step further: the side pockets. These were the huge pockets placed somewhere near the knee on the outer side of the trouser legs.

I remember the point when I realised how much of an absolute twat I looked in my Birmo's. I was with a friend named Francis – Fran for short – and we were both wearing our fave jumpers that had a big star in the centre. Our Birmo bags both had the side pockets and, as was the fashion, we had our hands in our pockets. As we walked, we caught our reflection in a clothing store mirror and it was fuckin' hideous!

We were both hunched over, with our hands in pockets as far down as our knees, walking with our legs apart like friggin' cowboys squaring up for a duel. We never wore Birmo's again, opting for our much more sensible white denim, tartan-hemmed Bay City Roller trousers instead.

CHAPTER NINETEEN

GERRY AND THE MERSEY FERRY

In the summer, as a treat, Mam and Dad used to take us on the ferry across the water to a place called New Brighton. When I was really little I'd think that we were travelling to another country, but later I found out it was only across to the other side of the River Mersey. The ferry would start off in the shadow of the Royal Liver Building, with those two majestic birds looking down on us from the traffic fume blackened buildings that have become an icon of the city I love. Mam was once a cleaner in the Royal Liver Building. She always used to tell us about its clock faces being twenty-five feet wide and how much larger they were than London's famous Great Westminster Clock (the one with Big Ben). Then she would tell us all about the Liver Birds that watched over the city and the Mersey; about the legend that says if the Liver Birds were to ever fly away, the city would crumble to dust.

Mam would also tell us about the grand spiral staircase,

where someone fell over, years before. Whenever we visited her at work, she used to say, 'Keep away from them stairs coz someone fell over the top and died.' It was a strange place to work as you weren't allowed to move anything, so my mam would have to clean and dust around objects and vases when wiping the tables.

We used to watch the ferry coming towards the landing dock and we'd lean forward so we could see the massive lorry tyres – that were strapped to the dockside and the boat – being squashed as the ferry pulled up alongside them. The ferryman would throw out a thick rope, which another man would slip over a metal post. Then he'd let the ramp down and everyone would pile out on to the ferry all at once. If I was there with mates, then we wouldn't have paid and would have to duck down in the middle of the clambering crowd and get on the ferry before we were noticed. We'd always be shitting ourselves as there was a rumour that some time ago the ferrymen caught three lads that hadn't paid their fare and tied their hands to ropes and pulled them back across the Mersey through the water. For this reason, we felt a whole lot better when we were on the ferry with Mam and Dad!

The journey across the River Mersey was an adventure in itself. I remember the ferry always smelling of thick oil and diesel fuel, and at that time the river didn't smell any better, so your stomach would be churning a little bit. Sometimes we would bug Mam to let us eat some of our sandwiches as we were crossing, along with a drink to wash the sandwiches down. We were almost always impatient for something and would never just wait until we arrived at the beach. Every now and then, Mam would cave because of the constant moaning and us saying we were hungry and thirsty, and she'd end up almost throwing the sandwiches at us. We'd sit there all content, looking out at the other side of the water, hoping the beach wouldn't be too packed, guzzling down our sandwiches.

I once did a horrible thing when we were on the ferry with my mates. I had some sandwiches, my friend Susan had a carton of milk, and we spotted some people sitting to one side, who had seasickness. So, I shoved a sandwich in my mouth, chewed it up, drank some milk and then swilled the milk and chewed the sandwich around in my mouth, mixing the two together. I started staggering around, like I was seasick, grabbing for the boat post to steady myself. Then I made a puking noise and spat the milk-sandwich mixture right out in front of them. Three of the people sitting there ended up vomiting, and although Susan almost peed her knickers laughing, I felt really sly. Not too sly to laugh though, and we were still laughing right up to the moment the ferryman grabbed me and Susan for bunking on the ferry without paying. That wiped the smile off our faces, especially when we realised the ferry we were on had a disco at the back.

I loved dancing, especially if I got to dance with a nice-looking lad. I could dance well, as could all my mates (it must have been all the practice we'd had shaking our arses in the NEMS music store). Back then, white lads couldn't dance to save their lives. Only the black guys knew how to dance, and they always looked so cool in the middle of the dance floor, spinning around with some girl while the white lads looked on.

The Mersey ferry was always rammed tight with families, but it got even worse when the song *Ferry Cross the Mersey* (by Gerry and the Pacemakers) became a hit because all the Scousers who had never bothered with the ferry suddenly wanted to see what Gerry was warbling on about; and this was still long before the tourist industry had started to kick in, so the only voices you would hear would be Scousers. As well as sounding the same, they would all be thinking the same thing: just how hard they were going to have to battle for a space on the New Brighton Beach. Buckets and spades, carrier bags full of sandwiches and lots of lemonade from the Alpine van were all you would be carrying, while the time-served beach visitors carried the odd deckchair too.

You would see lots of naughty-looking kids getting a pre-emptive clip round the earhole in advance of the serious pissing around they were planning to do when they got to the beach. Other kids would be getting a full-on slap in the gob for having pissed about already (back then you could slap, punch, or even drop-kick your kid without the little brat threatening to have you sued or locked up like they do nowadays). Then there was always the vomitor – the one kid who didn't need us to spit sandwich-and-milk combos at him/her. The mix of water-motion and diesel fumes would trigger projectile vomiting without any help from us! I always noticed that whenever there was a vomitor, they always vomited near the type of kids who would vomit at the slightest smell of vomit. So, all in all, we were happy to get to the other side of the river as too many kids being ill could start us all off.

Suddenly the ferry would hit the breaks (or reverse motors, or weigh anchor, or whatever the hell a boat does to stop going forward) and slow down so much that we'd almost fall over. This meant we were about to hit the other side. The tyres squash, the rope is thrown, the drawbridge thingy is about to come down and despite the ferryman calling for calm, everyone is trying to push their way to the front to be the first to disembark. It really was like a big free-for-all – everyone was bustled up, eagerly waiting for the ferryman to drop the gangway, while he was still being finicky and checking whether everyone was standing behind the metal strip so the gangway wouldn't hit them as it came down. The families pushing forward turned him into a man possessed as he stood waving his hands and shouting, 'Calm down! I'm doin' nothin' till you all calm down and get back!' We'd shuffle back like good little ferry-goers, nod our heads and stand patiently, as though standing in the school dinner queue. The ferryman would wait until everyone was calm and quiet. Then, as soon as the gangway had dropped down, it was like the Normandy Landings. Everyone would rush to get to the beach first – they all wanted the best spot and to have as much time on the beach as possible before they had to head back and catch the last ferry to Liverpool.

Me and Brian would play on the beach, collecting shells for Mam and building sandcastles that were the strangest and oddest shapes because we never had a bucket or spade. We'd use our hands and empty tins and cartons that we'd find on the beach. And we always got changed from our swimming gear behind a towel that Mam or Dad would hold up for modesty's sake.

I remember my mam kicking off when she saw some scruffbag of a mother letting her kid have a poo behind a really well-made sandcastle some kid had spent hours building. The woman waited for her kid to finish and just told him to throw some sand over it – the dirty bugger! I'll bet she was the same woman who let her dogs shit in the sandpit in Princes Park. Mam ended up grassing and telling the mam of the kid who built the sandcastle, and she kicked off on the woman. I laughed my head off at the whole thing just because it was funny watching Mam sneakily grassing on someone.

Me and Brian used to run right down the beach till we were almost out of eyesight, then we'd rush back to Mam for jam butties. If we were really lucky and had been good all day, we would be treated to some chips in a cardboard tray. I don't know why, but the chips in New Brighton tasted better than anywhere else in the world. For the life of me, I can't think why this was. They were always on the cold side and covered in sand that was blowing about the beach. I think they tasted that good because we were having a lovely day with the people we loved, in one of our favourite places on the planet. I mean, what food wouldn't taste good in that situation?

Those great days out always felt endlessly warm and sunny. I can remember sitting on the back of the ferry as we waved goodbye to New Brighton, wishing we could live there forever.

Sometimes, if me and my mates bunked on the ferry, we would just travel backwards and forwards from Liverpool to New Brighton and back without getting off, hiding in the toilets to avoid the ferryman sussing we didn't have tickets. That April, The Beatles had a hit with 'Ticket to Ride', which we used to call 'Free Ticket to Ride' on account of the free rides we had on the ferry.

I remember hanging out by the Pier Head quite a lot when I was around ten to eleven years old. My friends and I would jump the bus from by ours straight to the Royal Liver Building and then head down to our favourite little cafe on the corner. That cafe was a real 'greasy spoon', the type where you would have to wipe your knives and forks a few times before using them. We didn't eat any of the meals they served as there had been lots of complaints from people who got food poisoning. Instead, we used to get a cup of tea, a hot Oxo or a cup of Bovril. We were only kids, but back then, you were free to go wherever you wanted. There were no mobile phones so your mam could get in touch, but you really didn't need them because she had a gob that could shout for five postcodes. You could hear her shouting, 'Brian, Christine, get in!' like some bleedin' yodeller in the Alpines.

CHAPTER TWENTY

MUSEUMS, STATUES AND A BIT OF CULTURE

Liverpool Museum on William Brown Street (now called the World Museum) was where we used to go in the school holidays because it was free. It was also the place where me and Brian got to see the piece of moon rock. Everyone was queuing up to see this thing that had been brought all the way from space. I remember Brian being even more twitchy and animated than usual as we stood in the queue. When, finally, we were at the head of it, we stared through the glass case with our mouths hanging open. 'That's crap!' I said. 'It looks like a piece of one of the old houses near my nan's.' Our Brian nodded in agreement. We expected it to be bright and shiny, even glowing like the moon we saw in the night sky – this piece was really uninteresting, a piece of dull rock.

While the moon rock was a let-down, the mummies never were. I loved the mummies in the museum! I used to think to myself, how did they get permission to put real dead people into glass cases, just so we could have a nose at them? And how long was it before you were allowed to put a dead person on display? I'd stare at the multi-coloured jewels and polished stones that were either in the rings on the mummies' fingers or buried alongside them with their jewel-encrusted cups or other objects also encrusted with jewels. My mates all had shorter attention spans than me and a lot less imagination. They'd be telling me to hurry up as they were getting bored of looking at dead people, that they were getting off and if they left me on my own, the mummies might get me. I knew they were full of shite because the mummies would need metal fists to punch through glass that thick. Also, if they did come to life, the mummies would most probably go after them lot for saying they were boring.

One of the display cases that always caught my eye, and I think they've still got it there to this day, was the one with the mummy's hand. It was the hand of some queen or other that had beautiful gold rings on her fingers, but the hand looked like it was made of charcoal as it was jet-black with age. It fascinated me and at the same time scared the crap out of me as I'd seen an old movie with Peter Lorre called *The Beast With Five Fingers*. In it, there was a disembodied hand of a top pianist that came after all the people who were involved in the pianist's death and the hand killed every one of them. I used to think that if the glass wasn't as thick as it was, the hand might get out and kill the people who dug it up.

After the mummy browsing, we would go to the natural history part of the building, which is where they kept the live bugs. I used to be crapping myself, but I always put a brave face on in front of my friends. They had real tarantulas, scorpions and a variety of other killer spiders and insects that they kept behind sweaty, green-stained glass so moss- and slime-covered, you would have to go right up to it to see inside. Once you had your face pressed against the glass, you could see other bugs like rhino beetles, scarab beetles and the things that always made me feel a little sick…cockroaches! Not like the ones that might get in your house, the ones that always crunched when you stood on them. No, these were from some far-off land and they were massive. One of my mates, Col, told me that the reason they were so big was because the people who live where the cockroaches come from are so poor, they feed the cockroaches on poo, and then when they're fat enough (the cockroaches), they eat them. I remember going home that night and balking when trying to eat my dinner, because I couldn't get the thought of someone chomping on poo-filled cockroaches out of my mind.

A trip to the museum always followed the same route: mummies and ancient Egypt. Bugs and spiders, then the little alleyway was next. This consisted of a street lamp with mural photographs of a 1900s street. The murals would show families from that time sitting outside houses in the slums. The sound of kids from that period, as they played their Victorian games and laughed with each other, could be heard. This was always one of my favourite exhibits: it made you close your eyes and imagine you were back in time. A strange smell was added that you never smelt anywhere else you went to in your whole life.

The planetarium was next on the route. Now, this, to a kid, really was mind-blowing! You lay back and waited for the narration that would tell you everything about the universe while a display depicting the planets would project on to the ceiling. All the planets would move as the voice-over told you the details of each one. Then a shooting star would whizz across the sky... Tremendous!

Lastly, we would all leg it down into the basement to where all the old-fashioned street buggies and train carriages were. You could get into some serious trouble if you climbed on to the exhibitions and ran along inside the train carriages, like we did. Or, if you climbed into the street buggies, like we did also. I'm joking, of course: us being little angels, sensible and not naughty at all, would never do anything silly like that... honestly! In the same basement they had the first Ford car produced at the Ford factory at Halewood, a Ford Anglia 105E Saloon.

Having seen the parts of the museum that we liked the most, we would then head over to the Walker Art Gallery. When you entered the Walker, there was a fabulous painting – I think it was of the first horse ever to win the Grand National. As you went further in and to the right, there was a huge painting of Samson and Delilah over the staircase. It always disturbed me, the look of sheer pleasure and pure evil on Delilah's face as she held Samson's cropped-off hair and the scissors in her hands. I'd seen the film with Victor Mature and Hedy Lamarr and could never get my head around her doing that to the man she supposedly loved. On the right of the gallery entrance stairwell was a painting of Napoleon Bonaparte riding on a horse rearing up on its back legs, while he waved a sword in the air.

These fabulous paintings and the Roman sculptures in the sculpture room used to make me drift off into my own imagination. And I just couldn't believe that people like me, my nan and my mam and dad, ordinary human beings like us, could create things as mind-blowingly beautiful as the objects in front of me. I'd often catch a cold while staring because I only ever seemed to go into those buildings when it was raining and I'd usually be drenched through. God, I must have been nine, ten or eleven maybe. How cultured was I for a little sprog? Ha, ha! I suppose I was sick of being called thick at school, so I wanted to try and educate myself and get a little culture, even though at first I was just trying to get out of the rain. To see all those paintings made me awestruck. How the artists were able to make those works of art look so realistic was beyond me – they looked almost like photographs, but a lot more beautiful. So, I took a great interest in art and all things creative.

Outside the art gallery on the corner of Lime Street and William Brown Street there stood a huge column of sandstone, on the top of which was plonked a statue of the Duke of Wellington – who was very popular with pigeons because they all used to sit and poo on his head. We used to think that he was the guy who opened the very first welly-boot shop. At the base of the column was a carving of lots of soldiers who died in the Battle of Waterloo.

Just next to the column was the Steble fountain, a favourite with me and my mates. As wide as any fountain you could see, it had lots of metal statues of King Neptune and his mermaids. At the time we used to think that Neptune was real and must have had something to do with the guy on the column that made the welly boots, and maybe that's why there was a fountain, to test the boots in the water. As you've probably realised, we were a bit thick and hard of thinking at that time. Anyhow, we used to jump into the fountain whenever the weather was warm and we were down that end of town, no matter if we were wearing our school clothes, Sunday best or anything else. Soaked, all of us completely soaked, but instead of heading home and getting a hiding for ruining our clothes, we'd either go up to Victoria Street and climb all over the Victoria monument or we'd make a beeline for St George's Hall. One of Liverpool's most imposing buildings, it always looked like a Greek or Roman building from thousands of years ago, with its columns straight out of the Acropolis in Athens.

Because I had a creative mind that was always bubbling over with barmy ideas, I used to walk slowly up the St George's Hall steps in a world completely of my own, all the while imagining I was cautiously entering an ancient temple, where I might suddenly be attacked by a hydra with lots of heads, a minotaur with the head of a bull, or Medusa the Gorgon with her head of snakes – it never occurred to me at the time that most of my imagination had a head-like theme to it.

After my ancient monster jaunt, I'd join my mates by climbing on the giant lion statues that stood in front of St

George's Hall. The statues always reminded me of the lion from *The Lion The Witch And The Wardrobe*, which we once had read to us in my school, St Saviour's. The teacher at the time had large pictures to accompany the book so the kids at the back of the class could see. One of the pictures had a little girl walking along with the lion that was off to sacrifice himself to save all the creatures of Narnia, the land he ruled over. The classrooms back then were packed with kids and half of them started sobbing coz the story was so sad. But I didn't, because I wanted to walk with the lion with my hand on his mane, through a wood in a magical land. The lion's name was Aslan and the St George's Hall statues were exactly like him.

While my mates were kicking the lions or sitting on them, talking shit, I would straddle the back of one lion and pretend I was flying with it, right up until the moment the St George's security or some nosy bastard member of the public decided to geg (butt) in and order us down. We wouldn't give them any lip, though, not like the kids now; we just slipped away over to the statue of Major-General William Earle, who stood with his boots on Sudanese shields from a battle that the British won in Egypt in 1885. I always used to think he looked a bit smug for a guy who'd brought guns to a spear-and-shield battle, but it turns out the guns never did him much good anyway as he ended up getting killed anyway.

CHAPTER TWENTY-ONE

THAT'S ENTERTAINMENT!

As well as Liverpool turning out some of the most influential music of the twentieth century, it also provided the world with some of its best comedians. Ken Dodd, the wonderful Micky Finn – who became a close and dearly loved friend – Tom O'Connor, Stan Boardman, Kenny Everett, Jimmy Tarbuck, and the fabulous and absolutely crazy Freddie Starr. Oh, and me too, of course!

Micky Finn started off as a docker. Tom O'Connor was an ex-teacher and he was hysterical. Stan Boardman always told jokes about the Germans bombing our chippy. Jimmy Tarbuck actually worked for a television rentals company and Freddie Starr…well, he was a crazy star in his own right! Every single one of these comedians started life in the working men's clubs of Liverpool and finally got their big break on the numerous stages of the Liverpool theatres.

The theatres in Liverpool were always jam-packed. Ken

Dodd used to do his Spectacular at the Royal Court theatre, and I had the privilege of being one of his Diddy Men in the live shows.

As a kid, we didn't really get to go to the theatres that were dotted about all over Liverpool city centre. Now and then we might get to go and watch a pantomime of *Jack and the Beanstalk* or *Snow White*, or even *Aladdin* – if there were any cheap tickets going, or if an uncle or aunty was feeling particularly generous. We probably should have gone to see The Beatles perform at some time or other, but at that time they weren't the superstars they went on to become. To us, they were just local lads. I do regret not seeing the Fab Four in their heyday, but we never went to see musicians or concerts and the like, going to the pantomime was a lot higher on our list. We did used to hang around outside to see if we could get a peep at the singers though, especially if we had heard them singing on Nan's radiogram, or in NEMS music store, or even if we'd only seen their pictures in a music magazine.

One time we heard that The Jackson 5 were to perform on the Liverpool Empire situated by Lime Street station (the Empire was built in 1928 – that's for all you history buffs that get off on when theatres were built!). I loved listening to The Jackson 5, and they were one of the few groups I listened to that my nan approved of us playing on her radiogram – I think that was because they were kids and she didn't want to be seen saying that kids were crap or something.

Anyway, The Jackson 5 arrived in Liverpool in 1972, and to this day I don't know how the hell the group got in or out of the theatre because the whole of town was swarming with fans, exactly like when The Beatles first took off. All the bus lanes were backed up, but instead of complaining, most people got off the bus and joined the crowds that were pushing and shoving to try and get a glimpse of these world-famous child stars. We were in the thick of it, me and my mates, Susan and Janet, and almost red in the face from getting squashed, but it was all worth it when we saw Michael, the fourteen-year-old future King of Pop and his brothers, Jackie, Tito, Jermaine and Marlon.

We could see Jackie, Tito and Jermaine straight away – they were tall and towered above the swathe of adoring fans, but we could only make out the tops of Marlon and Michael's Afros as they were way younger and smaller than their brothers. Then someone propped them up on a podium and we caught a first glance of their amazing smiles – talk about an advertisement for toothpaste – me and my mates fell in love with the lot of them and started screaming like stupid ninnies. And I nearly shat myself when one minute it looked like Michael smiled and waved straight at me. Then the army of huge security guards ushered the boys into a limo and they sped away, followed by a mob of screaming girls, all tripping over each other. At that time if you could have had a favourite theatre, well, the Empire was mine, as it had had played host to a number of great artists, including Frank Sinatra, The Beatles and now, The Jackson 5.

The Everyman was another famous theatre in Liverpool. When the Everyman opened its doors in 1964, a friend and neighbour of my nan's, sitting in the living room of our flat, complained that Liverpool had enough theatres already and not nearly enough bingo halls! In later years, that neighbour and the rest of Liverpool would be glad that they did add another theatre instead of a bingo hall, as half of Liverpool's acting talent cut their teeth on The Everyman stage. Talent that included Bill Nighy, Alan Bleasdale, Willy Russell, Pete Postlethwaite and my old mate and film co-star, Julie Walters.

Me and my friends didn't hang around The Everyman and other famous theatres like the Playhouse, Neptune or the Unity, because most of what they showed went right over our heads – *King Lear*, operas and monologues just weren't appealing to us Scally kids. The only Scouse kids who went to watch proper theatre or classical musicals and ballets were those with parents who thought they were better than ours and wanted their kids to be cultured little snobs. In hindsight, though, me and me mates missed out on seeing some of Britain's finest performers doing some of their greatest and earliest performances: Anthony Hopkins and Patricia Routledge at the Playhouse, and Dame Judi Dench and Richard Burton at the Royal Court.

Another great Liverpudlian venue that stands right smack in between Liverpool's cathedrals on Hope Street is the Liverpool Philharmonic Hall. The 1930s iconic building is known these days for the 250 mostly classical events that it stages every year, but it was known to us kids back in the day for a very colourful song that went something like this:

In the Philharmonic Hall,
There are nudies on the wall,
And you get a funny feeling,
You could whitewash any ceiling,
Then your mind goes blank,
And you have to have a…

Well, you can guess the rest! Oh my God, did we used to giggle our heads off whenever we said the word 'nudie', because back then it was like a swear word to us kids so we would always be laughing when we sang it. We never giggled at the cruder words in the song because we never knew what they meant. The reason for the song was the large Art-Deco frieze of naked women on the walls of the Philharmonic concert hall. Not that we ever saw them because 'the Phil' – as it was then and is still known – was off-limits to little kids who might take the piss out of the decor.

To be honest, we never wanted to go in, we were happy to imagine what the walls looked like, while singing the dirty song. Although we did pretend to try and enter through the front glass doors every now and then, just to see the doorman's face turn red as he ran backwards and forwards between doors, trying to keep us menaces out.

I did finally get to see the fabled nudies of the Philharmonic Hall but it was many years on from us winding up the Philharmonic doorman. At twelve, my school – Paddy Comprehensive – took eight of us on a cultural trip to hear the Philharmonic Orchestra play some classical music from the world's most-loved classical pieces and opera arias. Our teacher was thrilled to be going on the visit and kept droning on about how the Philharmonic Orchestra is the only one in Great Britain to have its own hall and is the longest-surviving professional orchestra in the country... Boring! At least that's what we all decided in our class for the hard of thinking, but as this was a bit of a break from our everyday thicko lessons, we went along without too much fuss.

I have to admit that seeing the nudies at the Phil could have taken away from the music I was about to experience, as could my talkative friend giving me a history lesson on the cinema screen that rises up from the stage whenever they showed a film. Thankfully, the nudies and my chatty mate were overshadowed by the sound of the orchestra as they started to play. Everything was music; it filled every space in the hall and every thought in my mind. And the music was so beautiful, even though I didn't know what it was and I couldn't believe that normal people that you might bump into in the street could come together and make a sound like I was listening to.

Ten minutes into the concert, I had completely blocked out everything but the music. I didn't even have any peripheral vision as my eyes were fixed on the orchestra, even though I knew that my mate and other classmates were messing around, not concentrating at all. Then I heard a music piece that I recognised – I think it was from *The Nutcracker Suite* – and this made me feel almost like I had a right to be there, like I was getting onto something my mates just couldn't understand, although my friend did start humming along when they played the *Dance of the Sugar Plum Fairy* – silly cow!

I was glad the school took us to the Phil that day because it opened my eyes to a different music I wasn't used to hearing. Not that I'd have run out and bought myself a classical music record – any money for records would have gone on whichever group or singer was topping the charts – but I did appreciate that you can like any type of music at all, you just had to listen long enough to hear what piece takes your fancy.

After the concert we piled out of the Philharmonic and across the road to the pub of the same name. We were thrilled when the teacher said that we were going into the pub so we had to be on our best behaviour. I was thinking the same as all my classmates – booze! Not that any of us had ever really tasted alcohol – with the exception of the swig of brandy your parents gave you at Christmas, which you quickly spat out in the kitchen sink. But the thought of us going into a real pub surrounded by beer and darts and smoke was akin to going into a cave full of treasure. The teacher then started giving us a boring history lesson, saying that the pub was built in the late nineteenth century and designed by Walter Thomas, but not Walter Aubrey Thomas, designer of the Royal Liver Building. Our teacher thought this fact was hilarious and he giggled like a big kid. Our attention was elsewhere as we had discovered the Phil pub's large entrance gates that were – to quote my teacher – Art Deco in style. He didn't mention that these gates were perfect for climbing and swinging on.

'Get off, now!' our teacher screamed at us. 'Stop acting like idiots!'

Idiots? We were in the school's idiot class, what did he expect?

Inside the pub we were met by a cloud of smoke that made us all cough a little. All eyes were on us as our teacher said 'Hi' to the bar staff and then led us across the pub. 'Children, notice the musical themed panels around the walls,' he remarked. 'It's interesting that they are made from repoussé copper…' Nah, our attention wasn't on whatever our teacher was droning on about, it was on two lads – usually quiet classmates – trying to steal drinks from a table, where two old men had been sitting. One of the lads managed to have a quick swig from a pint glass, but the other was immediately spotted.

'Fletcher! Don't you dare!' yelled the teacher causing the lad, Barry Fletcher, to immediately drop the glass he was holding. Luckily, it didn't smash or we would have been told to leave there and then. The teacher's face turned plum red as he tensely whispered something into Fletcher's ear. He then took a deep breath and asked us to follow him. We were all in awe of the two lads, especially the one who managed to have a drink and never got caught. I will just make a point of this, that the lad's name was Ian Johnston and from that day forward, he was a legend in our school.

The day at the two Philharmonics (hall and pub) got really weird when our teacher said, 'I'm going to check that nobody is using the toilets before we go in.' And then he walked into the men's toilets. Not one of us said a word, we all just frowned suspiciously. Our teacher emerged from the toilets, thanking two men who were walking behind him… Very suss! It turned out that our teacher had asked the men if they could vacate the toilet so us kids could go in.

'Sir, that's the boys' toilet,' I said, confused.

'I'm not going in the boys' bog!' said my chatty mate.

'Sir, Christine's okay to go in coz she's a man!' said a lad who normally sat quietly at the back of our class and who later got a punch in the throat, the cheeky little shit!

We followed the teacher into the toilets and he give us a quick lecture on what it was we were looking at, while every now and then asking a punter who was in need of a piss if he could not come in and instead wait outside a moment. 'Children, note the urinals are made from a wonderful roseate marble…'

Okay, nowadays I get it; the toilets are the last of their kind and beautiful in their construction blah, blah, blah, but back then, I didn't get it at all. The toilets were just fancy toilets. I hadn't been in any other adult toilets so who was to say they weren't all like these toilets? Also, one of the men our teacher had forced from the loo had obviously unloaded a few pounds because the smell in there was grossly disgusting and making us all gag.

Gagging aside, it was a good day out. We swung on Art Deco gates and pissed our teacher right off, we got to see a pink marble smelly toilet, a legend was born in the form of Ian Johnston, and I finally got to see the fabled Philharmonic nudies.

CHAPTER TWENTY-TWO

SPACE HOPPING

As a kid I loved playing outside in the three parks, the streets of Liverpool 8 and the tenements that we lived in. Most of the time Mam and Dad couldn't get me to come in because I was like a feral street urchin who needed to bask in the cold sunlight and the not-so-fresh Liverpool fresh air. However, when I had a new toy of some description my parents couldn't prise me away from it, no matter who came knocking for me to play out. With a new toy, the only chance I might play out was if Mam and Dad let me take it outside with me. They never did because it might get stolen or broken, so I would just sit in the living room, playing for days on end.

The sixties toys were the best because toy-making was just coming into its own. The manufacturers no longer had to use metal to make the toys, and plastic ones were a lot cheaper, which meant there was a hell of a lot more choice.

The toys that I remember the most were Etch A Sketch, Sindy, View-Master, Play-Doh, Spirograph, KerPlunk and Scalextric. I remember I had an Etch A Sketch that I was really crap at. On the telly, they showed adverts with kids using Etch A Sketches and turning out amazingly detailed pictures of Venice or the Mona Lisa. Me, I could barely etch out a sketch of a stick man! Spirograph was much better because as long as you could hold a pencil, you could make the most wonderful patterns and flowery shapes. My friends at the time used to sit in our living room totally silent, tongues sticking out of one side of their mouths, completely engrossed in what they were drawing – 'Pass us a different shape, Crissy,' were all the words you might get out of them. Then we would have the big reveal to my mam and Nan and be so proud showing off the patterns we'd created, patterns we thought were unique to us, until we realised that ours were the very basic starting out patterns.

Considering my mam, dad and nan never had two pennies to rub together they always seemed to get the popular toys for us, even if it was a few years after the toys were popular. The View-Master was the only toy that was a favourite with the whole family, including Nan, and that was because we had about ten picture reels to go with it. Two of the reels showed funny scenes from the TV show, *The Addams Family*. One had scenes from the *Batman* television series. And all the other reels showed amazing waterfalls, Egyptian monuments and mummies, and capital cities from around the world.

The toy that me and our Brian shared was Play-Doh, and

we kept playing with it until the bright pink of it turned completely mud coloured. There was something about the smell of Play-Doh that made us sit there sniffing it for hours on end, like we were both cokeheads; nothing else on the planet smelled like it. I can never remember us making anything good out of the Play-Doh the way we made things out of plasticine, but we didn't give a shit because it smelled great.

Brian's favourite toy was Action Man and although they used to show a kid with more than one Action Man on the TV ads, one was all our Brian would ever own. Action Man came out in the mid- to late-sixties, but Brian only got one in 1970. When Brian got an action story in his head, that could be anything from Action Man having to traverse a ravine to defuse a bomb and then dive off a cliff into the ocean, or him having to charge his way through the jungle of a lost island to do battle with a forty-foot-high human being-devouring ape. He would move all the furniture around just to give his Action Man the kind of terrain he might need to carry out his suicide missions. Nan used to walk into the living room, take a deep breath and slowly arrange the furniture back to the way it was. My mam used to shout if Brian was going over the top and bringing bits of furniture from the bedroom for his action landscape. Dad used to join in with Brian and help make the terrain, because he was just a big kid at heart.

The Space Hopper came out in time for my thirteenth birthday. It was the toy I wanted more than any toy I had wanted my whole life (apart from a Chopper bike, that is). I had dreams about getting a Space Hopper and I had nightmares about not getting a Space Hopper, that's how crazy I was about them. 'Stop going on about stupid Space Hoppers, will ya!' That's what my mates used to say, but I knew that the ones who were saying it stood no chance of getting one themselves because their birthdays weren't coming up, so they were just jealous in case I did get one. Boy, did I hint and go on and on to my mam and Dad about that bleedin' toy! And there was no way I should have been as surprised as I was when they eventually caved in and got me one.

Orange! That's what I saw peeping out from behind the couch on the morning of my thirteenth birthday. Dad had tried wrapping it but it was too big, so Mam eventually put a blanket over it, but that had fallen off. But I did not give a hoot: I had a Space Hopper, whether it was wrapped or not.

'If you're going in the street with it, don't go over any glass or it'll pop!' said my dad.

'Don't go bouncing too high or your skirt will fly up and the boys will see your knickers!' said Mam.

I nodded at anything they said as I stood in awe of the strange orange object. I remember not actually sitting on it for some strange reason, not until I got out into the street. Mam and Dad followed me and had to hold back their laughter when my first bounce attempt sent me arse over tit, almost doing a face-plant into the pavement. The next attempt saw me bouncing off along the street, with all the neighbourhood kids following me like they were enchanted by the power of the magical orange ball.

I could never tell if the things you held onto at the top of the Space Hopper's head were ears or horns – I liked to think they were ears otherwise it would have felt like I was riding a demon or something. John Daniels and his sister Mo, Tracy what's-her-face (I can't remember her second name) and her two sisters, and a big lad called Paul were the only neighbourhood kids I let have a go on my Space Hopper. John, because he was really funny and everyone liked him. Mo, Tracy and her sisters, because we hung around together. And Paul, because he had a catapult that he said he'd shoot the Space Hopper with unless I gave him a go. (Paul actually turned out to be a good friend of mine and Brian's, and he even made Brian a catapult of his own.)

I never popped that Space Hopper, no matter what gravel and glass I bounced over – it was made of super rubber or something like it. When I did get a little bored of it, which was a few years after I should have done, I gave my wonderful Space Hopper friend to my best friend's niece. She burst the Space Hopper in the first week of bouncing on it because – and I'm never one to mention a person's weight – she was a huge fat cow who consumed anything edible within a five-mile radius. I can remember wanting to deck her when I found out she'd popped my orange friend but, as I said, she was huge and probably would have battered me, sat on me, or barbecued and ate me, the Space-Hopper-killing bint!

Just recently, I was looking on eBay and came across lots of sixties and seventies toys. Straight away, I spotted an original Spirograph, a Chopper bike – that was a little worse for wear

– and an authentic Space Hopper from back in the day, still in mint condition. Did I buy any of them? All of them? I'll let you work that one out.

CHAPTER TWENTY-THREE

THE EXTENDED FAMILY

One thing that was very common in Liverpool when I was little was the amount of non-related relatives you would have. They could be neighbours or best friends of your mam or dad, or auntie or uncle, they could be someone that your dad plays darts with down the pub on a Saturday night, or they might even be someone your mam once stood next to in the bag wash. These unrelated acquaintances would be known as your aunts or uncles. We, me and my brothers, grew up with loads of aunts and uncles.

'Your Aunt Pat's calling later, so tidy up your mess!' my mam would say.

'I'm off out with your Uncle Bernie for a pint!' I heard my dad say on more than one occasion.

We thought our grandparents on both sides must have bred like rabbits for the sheer amount of kids they must have had! But how were we to know they weren't relatives? I mean, every one of their kids was your cousin. I didn't mind though as it meant that we had a lot more friends to play with, and if there was any trouble you would have a lot of backup. Another plus about having these so-called aunties and uncles, they used to give you little presents all the time, or buy you sweets and stuff whenever they saw you in the street. I think this was because the false relatives felt like they had something to prove, while the real ones took us for granted and give us sod all.

The only bad thing about the false relatives was that they also felt they should invest more time in teaching you the rights and wrongs of life. If they saw me doing the slightest thing wrong, they would bollock me out even more than my real aunties and uncles, or they'd give me a good hard slap whenever they saw me pissing about like an idiot, doing something I really shouldn't be doing. And they were bigger grasses than your real aunties and uncles too, always running back to my mam or Nan with some info about me and my mates smashing a window or scratching a car. Or they'd be sitting off with my dad in the pub, giving him a full list of the crap I'd done while knocking a couple of pints back.

'What's this your Uncle Jimbo told me that you were smashing bombdie windows on Parliament Street the other day, soft girl?' my dad would say.

'Who's Uncle Jimbo? We haven't got an Uncle Jimbo,' I'd say.

'Me belt's coming off!' he'd say.

'Oh, Uncle Jimbo! Yes, we did smash a few windows to stop the vandals smashing them,' I'd say.

'No playing out for you tonight, smart arse!' he'd say.

To sum up, my false relatives were always putting me in the shit.

CHAPTER TWENTY-FOUR

THAT'S THE SOUND OF THE POLICE

The police in the early sixties worked mostly on foot patrol. The cars they did have were old, black, post-war vehicles, and the occasional Jaguar Mark 2 for the upper crust of the police department. You'd always see the police walking in twos, just like on TV, with their hands behind their backs. Usually one of the two would carry a long stick that he would tap on the pavement and walls, causing all the pub owners that had illegal stay-behinds to hush their punters, saying, 'Keep quiet, the coppers are outside!' as they could hear the stick knocking. But in 1964–65 Kirkby in Liverpool saw its very first Panda police cars. Mostly Ford Anglias, they were blue and white in colour. They used to call them 'Pandas' because of the television show *Z Cars*, which was shown without colour and always made the cars look like they were painted black and white. Legend has it that the shade of blue used for the cars was chosen because the Chief Constable of Lancashire went to either Oxford or Cambridge University, and blue was the college colour.

The Panda cars changed the way our streets were patrolled. As these were affordable cars, the police issued them to a lot of officers and so there were less police walking the beat and they became more and more detached from the public. The first time I saw a Panda car was when it was chasing a gang of lads across a road near my nan's. Two of the lads – dead ringers for John Lennon and Paul McCartney – were cornered, so they dived over a garden wall and shoved two fingers up at the police. Ten minutes later, I saw one of the other lads going past in the back of the police Panda car almost in tears, and he looked like Ringo. Of all the look-alike Beatles they could have caught, it had to be poor bloody Ringo!

The police always had a weird relationship with the Liverpool public, especially around the inner-city areas, where there were housing estates, clubs and a multi-cultural community.

When I lived with Nan in Windsor Gardens we would have to pass our Aunty Winnie's flat to get to the main stairwell, but my mam didn't want us passing by Winnie's because her husband was a policeman and, according to Mam, if you had a husband who was a policeman then you were a snitch, a rat, a grass! She was convinced that even if you didn't want to be a grass, if you had a policeman husband then sooner or later, you would become a grass. Mam said if Winnie found something out about someone that she knew doing something illegal then it was bound to come out some time in conversation, and even if the conversation wasn't with her husband, he would probably be listening in by the door, like the police do.

We were convinced by Mam's logic, however, we were willing to risk arrest if it meant we could pass by Winnie's flat and not have to take the long route up the stairs, along and then down to the main staircase. Mam used to say, 'I'll find out if you went past their flat!' So, we avoided Winnie's, and if and when we did see her, we would try not to give her anything our policeman uncle would find incriminating.

The police weren't well liked in our household or anywhere in the area either. They were the enemy, at least that was the case right up until someone broke into your house or you needed their help. I think that the dislike stemmed from what my nan once called *the bad eggs*. These were the police that were bad people before they joined, and would be bad until and after they retired; the type of police that would drive past me and me mates and give my mates bad looks, just because they were from Granby Street and more often than not black, Chinese, Indian or Arab. When I was little, I didn't notice it as much, as even the bad police didn't want to be seen picking on little kids. But as I got older, I did notice that we – me and my racially diverse friends – were getting a lot more attention. You would see the police cars coming along the street and you could tell when they spotted us because they would slow down and come closer to the kerb. I wouldn't have minded if we were carrying swag bags and had on striped jumpers with black masks, but most of the time we would be dressed in school uniform and just heading home for tea.

'Where are you lot going?' the bad eggs would say out of the car window.

'I hope you girls aren't getting up to no good,' was what the nicer police might say if they wanted to warn you without being nasty. But it was the bad eggs that stuck in your mind, not the local bobby on the beat, and so you would grow up with a natural fear of the police. My friends would grow up with less fear and more hate through the amount of times the police treated them less fairly than the white girls in our gang. The police treating them this way gave a green flag to the racist elements in our city to do the same. If the police weren't going to treat the people from diverse backgrounds with the same level of respect as everyone else then this meant that the racists could get away with abusing them, as the police obviously wouldn't give a shit. The result of this would be a division, with gangs of white and black, skinheads and Afros having a gang war that would turn into a riot, right next to where I lived.

The Falkner Square estate was just across from where I'd lived with my nan, mam and dad in Windsor Gardens. The residents of the estate were mostly black, mixed race and usually born in Liverpool. Now, Liverpool 8 being a ghetto, you might think that skinheads and other races would have to travel across the city to get there so they could carry out their attacks on the people of the area, but no, the skinheads lived in Toxteth, some of them right in the heart of Windsor Gardens. Mostly, the skinheads who started the race riots of 1972 were from the Dingle and areas around the outskirts of Toxteth.

The first night it all kicked off there was a big gang of skinheads and other white guys who probably wanted to be skinheads, but liked having long hair – 'tossers', I'd call them. These tossers attacked the Falkner housing estate by running through, shouting and screaming all kinds of racist stuff, while carrying sticks, chains, knives and bottles to hit the people who lived there. They started smashing windows and street lamps, then attacking anyone at all who was walking through the estate, whether they lived there or were just passing through.

I remember going into the estate with a lad friend of mine. At the time I was living in Chatsworth Street, which was only a five-minute walk from the Falkner estate. The lad – let's call him Robbo – walked me through the estate and, as we walked, I was shocked to see all the broken bottles and the smashed windows being boarded up. I was also very surprised that there were no police to be seen. It was like they had turned a blind eye to the events of the previous night. I remember seeing a woman that I always saw, distressed and walking around the area – usually talking to herself and swearing at cats – and she was sitting on the bottom of some steps crying, and I had never seen her cry before then, no matter how distressed she got. It is strange the things that stick out in a kid's mind.

So, I went to my mate's house and his mam gave us biscuits and tea, but she never mentioned what had gone on until I was leaving: 'I hope you won't be going out tonight, love,' she said, with a look of worry on her face. 'Those lot haven't finished, so you watch yourself.' 'Those lot' were the skinheads, the racists, and some of the black guys who also looked for trouble and enjoyed kicking off. The guys I saw building barricades as I was on my way home that day weren't the troublemakers, they were the guys who were concerned for the wellbeing of the families who lived on the Falkner estate. The guys who knew that because of their ethnicity and that of their families and neighbours, the police support they could expect to help them protect their homes was non-existent. So, they had to take matters into their own hands and barricade against the attack they knew would come.

The skinheads attacked that night but, thankfully, the barricades held them off. Over the next few days, the barricades were taken down in the daytime and re-erected in the evening, and even though the skinheads showed up, they couldn't get by the barricades. What happened next reinforced the hatred for the police in Toxteth: the police told the people in the Falkner estate to remove the barricades. The guys said 'Piss off' in so many words, as would anyone who was going to be attacked. And so there was a riot and the police charged at the barricades, doing the skinheads' job for them. In fact, the skinheads looked on, laughing amongst themselves as the police attacked the barricades.

The barricades finally fell to the police and as they got into the estate they made a few arrests, but for the most part the lads who built the barricades and defended the estate against the skinheads' onslaught were given refuge by the people who lived there. People who appreciated what these guys had actually done: protected their homes and their children.

We could hear the screams and racist chants even from

where we lived and it almost had me crying. Why the fuck would people, neighbours, Scousers behave in this way? The next day, while visiting one of my Windsor Gardens mates, I saw three skinheads arguing with two Caribbean families on one of the landings, and the worst thing was I recognised the skinhead lads who were being racist. The lads got chased by the Caribbean family and their white neighbours because their hate wasn't wanted in the tenements.

I'd managed to avoid being a part of what was happening that year, but I was sympathetic to those who lived on the Falkner estate and those who were suffering in Windsor Gardens too. I think I really felt for them because of what had happened to me some years before. I was with three friends and our Brian down near the David Lewis children's club, near the bottom of Upper Parliament Street. We'd been to the club to play table tennis and pool, and were now on our way back because Brian was twitching, which meant he was hungry. My mates were two Arab girls and one white girl. We had just crossed over when we heard 'N****r lover!' When we turned around, we saw a group of skinheads wearing Doc Marten boots, jeans and black Harrington jackets. The thing that surprised me before I felt any fear was that they were shouting 'N****r lover' at me and I was with two Arab girls. The only time I'd heard that racist word shouted was when it was aimed at the mixed race and black guys in the area.

'Dickheads!' I shouted back at the skinheads. My mates had that 'What the fuck are you doing?' look on their faces, but I continued shouting because they – the skinheads – were shouting at me. 'You cheeky baldy bastards!'

That was it; the skinheads ran over and kicked the shit out of us. We had a go at fighting back, but like all bullies and racists, these dickheads had a gang backing them up and they were a lot older than us. Our Brian even pulled his plastic cowboy gun on them and demanded they stop hitting us. Luckily, this added a bit of levity to the situation and while the skinheads were pissing themselves laughing, we got away.

We were all traumatised after that horrible encounter. For one, I couldn't understand how a group of big lads could beat up some girls and a lad who were a lot younger than them. For two, how could they call me that racist name when I was with Arab girls? I just couldn't work it out. Some years later, I did work it out: skinheads and racists aren't the smartest people in the world and having to work out a person's ethnicity is totally beyond their fuckin' tiny brains, therefore, they group anyone non-white, regardless of racial heritage.

I have to add a little footnote to this story and that's just to say that not all the skinheads I ever met were racists or thugs. The music a lot of them listened to was Caribbean-influenced Ska and Reggae and therefore the clubs they went to were a mix of black and white punters. So, like the bands around at the time, the skinheads had both black and white members in their gangs. As Hans Christian Andersen said, 'Where words fail, music speaks'

CHAPTER TWENTY-FIVE

BOMMIE NIGHT

B onfire Night was amazing for us kids. We used to start
collecting wood weeks before the actual night and each
tenement or estate would have its own bonfire wood that all
the big lads used to keep guard over. This was to make sure
nobody from a rival estate stole the wood or set fire to it out
of pure jealousy. The closer it got to the date, the bigger the
fights were that broke out between rival wood collectors.

There was a lot of pride in having the best bonfire. Some
would be built as high as fifteen to twenty feet. Others were
small, but a lot wider. It had to have some sort of proper
organising or else the firemen would turn up and dowse your
fire with water. There was none of this fuckin' nonsense you
get nowadays from kids throwing bricks at the firemen. The
only thing we used to throw on the fire was potatoes. We
loved those hot potatoes, but it was risky trying to retrieve
them from the fire. When you did, someone might shout,

'Get back! Get back!' because you could guarantee there was someone else throwing a can of paraffin, petrol or firelighters onto the fire, followed by a loud explosion.

The run-up to Bonfire Night was the most fun, what with collecting old doors, bits of trees, window frames and anything else that might burn, and getting congratulated by the big lads when we turned up with all we had found. Also, as the real name for Bonfire Night was Guy Fawkes Night, we'd always have our Ian in his pram, dressed up as the 'guy'. We would stand outside Ali's sweet shop, asking for pennies from anyone who passed and trying to convince people that we'd made our Ian from old rags.

'Penny for the guy, mister?'

'Penny for the guy, missus?'

The passers-by would take one look at our Brian dressed like who-knows-what and start laughing. Great! We knew that those who laughed always gave the most money. We would be outside Ali's every night for about a week before the big night, and we would make lots of money, which we used to spend on sweets and chocolate; the three of us eating as many sweets as possible before heading home.

One Bonfire Night, Mum stopped us from going down to our tenement bonfire. 'You're not going down there while all those idiots are throwing bangers,' she said. 'Get some chairs and you can stand on them and look over the landing.' At this point we were crying and kicking off: 'No! We wanna go down there!' we shouted. So my mam appeased us by getting us some sparklers to play with. This immediately shut us up and we were more than happy to follow her Health and Safety rules, waving our sparklers while watching the bonfire below. Unfortunately, someone let off a rocket directly below our landing, which shot up and hit me right in the forehead. Thirty minutes later I was in the hospital alongside lots of other firework-related casualties. To this day, I've still got that scar – so much for staying bleedin' safe!

Sometimes we used to go to see the fireworks and watch the bonfire at one of the big parks, Wavertree Park, or sometimes Newsham Park – which had the largest firework display – because they were well organised and there was no chance of a knobhead shooting me in the head with a rocket! The fireworks at those events had the largest explosions and seemed to fill up the whole sky with more colours than any rainbow. And the noise of the explosions was ear-shattering. We'd all stick our fingers in our ears, but you could still hear the 'Bang! Boom! Bang!' of the fireworks, no matter what you did. You could always hear the little kids who were watching start to cry because the fireworks were too loud for their delicate ears.

CHAPTER TWENTY-SIX

WORK, MONEY AND THE LACK THEREOF

I mentioned in the introduction to this book that I was going to give a mishmash recollection of my experiences growing up in sixties and seventies Liverpool. Well, this chapter is where the mish well and truly meets the mash. Money was always a difficult subject in our house because we never seemed to have any. So we – children and parents alike – were forced to save where we could and make money in any way we could. The following chapter has so many examples I was just going to write a list and let your imagination fill in the details. Then my publisher kindly reminded me that if I did this, I'd have to add to that list 'Not getting paid by my publisher for writing a book that has lists instead of details'. So, here come the details, some of which are short like this: When we had the Egg and Spoon race in school, we weren't allowed to take eggs in case they smashed because we couldn't afford to waste food. So me and Brian were the only kids in school who never competed in the Egg and Spoon. And some of which are long, like this...

While The Beatles were leading the charge of the British Invasion of America, back home, the city was experiencing its first real period of decline. Liverpool's once thriving docklands, the heartlands of our mighty port city, became a victim of the times, as the advent of containerism, the subsequent laying off of the dock workforce and the strikes that followed hit the city full-on in the gut. For us kids this was a bloody pain because the strikes meant we had no money for clothes so we had to wear welly boots, not just through the winter, but right through the summer months too, which meant a lot more welly-rash. As well as year-round wellies, we also got the school-grant coat, which was a duffle coat with no lining, that was made from some kind of felt material and was freezing cold in the winter months.

I remember on Copperas Hill, the street between the Vines pub and the Adelphi hotel in Liverpool's city centre, if you walked up the hill to where the taxi rank was on your right, there was a black door that led to the offices of the UAB (Unemployment Assistance Board). This was where you were sent for clothes when your parents had no money. The UAB would supply you with coats and whatever else you needed. Me and our Brian got a black gabardine mac each. I remember we were so happy, tying our big belts and checking out who looked the best. My brother thought he looked like some kind of cool private eye, a gumshoe, Sam Spade, like a miniature Bogart or something. I thought he looked more like bloody Colombo myself! And so we both had a big posh gabardine mac each, while our toes were sticking out of threadbare wellies.

Great Homer Street Market – also known as 'Greatie Market' – was a lifesaver in leaner times because they sold everything dirt cheap, and everything you could ever think to buy. The whole place was a huge collection of stalls, each heaped high with the cheapest products on the market. What I remember them selling most of all were shoes – hundreds and hundreds of different types, styles and colours. Some leather, some plastic, and some that turned out to be like cardboard, which would immediately fall to bits, having got the slightest bit moist. The shoes were all strung together by their laces – to stop people stealing them –yeah, right – and you had a struggle trying them on because as you pulled one from the table, a train of others followed.

The worst thing about Greatie Market shoes was the price. Nah, I'm not talking about the actual cost, I mean the price scrawled on the sole of the shoe in black permanent marker, in letters large enough to put on a friggin' billboard. For the most part, no one would ever see the price, but as soon as you knelt down in school assembly to say prayers, or you climbed up on something, then everyone would suss out where you'd got your shoes from and just how trampy-cheap they were. The kids would say, 'Eeeh, you little scav! You've been to Greatie Market! What a bad tramp!' and no matter how hard you denied it, the proof was there in mega-large letters on the soles of your shoes. I remember legging it home and pouring as much Jif scouring powder onto the soles as I could, then scrubbing like hell to get the price off, to the sound of The Beatles' first hit, 'Love Me Do'.

Another consequence of the strikes, besides not being able to afford decent clothing, was the bad blood between families and friends when some refused to follow the strike and instead became scabs, breaking the lines and going into work. I remember overhearing my mam and dad talking about two brothers, who had worked together on the docklands, suddenly going their own ways when it came to the strikes: one stayed working, the other stayed with the majority of workers on strike. Those two brothers never spoke to each other ever again. This kind of feud was rare but it did happen as a result of the city being hit so hard. To be fair, it must have been hard whatever side of the argument you were coming from: if you had a large family who needed the income, what choice would you have but to keep working? The heartache it caused was horrible and almost tore the city in two. Those returning to work felt like scum as they were booed and cursed at, called 'Scab' and spat at as they turned up to do the same job they and their accusers had stood side by side doing, only weeks before. But as I said, there are people to this day – families, and those who were once friends – who still don't speak to each other because of those terrible days of the dockland strikes.

Liverpool has always been a political city, I suppose. I was brought up in a pro-Labour household, although I didn't have a clue what Labour was. My mother voted Labour, her mother voted Labour, and we were told to vote Labour when we grew up because, and I quote my mam here, 'Women died so that you could vote!' The city had been Labour since day dot. Our household could have been described as a socialist one, as was the whole city, because we looked after each other in good times and bad.

In those leaner times my dad would have to find work where he could get it. He often changed jobs, as employment wasn't assured for any fixed period of time. Dad worked as a street sweep in the sixties, and as a bin man, and then as a sewer man down the grids in the seventies. As a bin man, he went through a phase of bringing home any old junk that he found in the bins, or on the tips, as he went about his job, day to day.

'One man's shite is another man's treasure,' he'd say. An attitude we were all glad he changed when he became a sewer man. He used to be out of the house before it got light and then he'd be back with a big grin on his face, carrying a load of stuff you'd think he was about to throw out. 'Margie, got a surprise for you!' he'd shout, thinking my mam was gonna come running to meet him and jump up and down on the spot, clapping her hands like an excited puppy. She would walk into the room and raise an eyebrow, followed by a look of disgust – you know, the kind of look you have when you're about to change a baby's nappy, but you're unsure if it's a number one or two? But Dad would be undeterred and still excited as she opened whatever it was he'd covered up, so he could sneak it out of the depot. My mam used to say that the depot should be paying Dad for taking away the shit he was bringing into our house, never mind him having to hide it! Then it was the big reveal, what had he brought home? More plastic fruit, or another painting of 'Tina', a half-dressed dusky maiden by the artist J.H. Lynch. We had lots of those cheap paintings, with their white plastic frames, along with paintings of a stern-looking Asian woman that were always in hues of pale green and blue. We even had a table with the painting of the Asian lady as the table top.

Then there were my mam's pet hate paintings, the crying children with the wide eyes. She said these paintings were cursed: 'Do not be bringing them in here!' she used to say. 'They'll burn the friggin' house down!' I wasn't sure what she meant by them 'burning the house down' as the pictures weren't exactly wired up to the leccy. Dad found it hilarious that she was superstitious, and so I think, secretly, he was bringing the crying kid pictures home to deliberately tick her off – 'If you have to bring the crying boy, then get the bleedin' crying girl too!' she would say. Mam believed that these crying kids cancelled out the curse if you hung one of each sex on the walls opposite each other.

Dad did eventually bring home a crying girl painting to go with the shedload of crying boy paintings we had stashed behind the couch, but my mam still refused to hang them. The only thing Dad liked bringing home more than plastic framed paintings was plastic fruit. Not just oranges, apples, lemons and grapes, but fruit you couldn't recognise because it was from foreign places. Mam actually liked the plastic fruit because it brought lots of colour to the living room, and I think she secretly liked it because it was the one impractical, fuckin' useless thing we had that wasn't gonna burn the house down.

Whenever I saw Dad turn up with the exotic plastic fruit I used to wonder just how far his bin route took him. Was he crossing continents? You would have thought so by the strange plastic fruit in our house. My mam used to keep the 'British' fruit in a bowl on the table in case the other exotic plastic fruit confused visitors. To her, bananas and Seville oranges were English because you didn't have to go to Granby Street's international stores to buy them. I remember once our Brian moved the table with the Asian lady painting on so he could play with his toys. He moved it too close to the fire and the British fruit on the table melted. Mam said, 'You've singed me bloody bananas!' and she was stuck with having to display the exotic fruit for weeks after, which – in truth – she didn't mind as it became a conversation starter.

While my mam was fussy about what junk Dad brought into the house, he was always happy with whatever he found when he worked on the bins. Manky old dolls, cutlery, toys and all kinds of nasty stuff… to him, anything that looked like it might be a good find *was* a good find.

Nan had seen much poorer times in her lifetime and she used to let us all know it. Whenever we complained about not having new shoes, or the plastic British fruit had melted, she would remind us just how bad it was when she was growing up. She used to say, 'You lot don't even know you're born!' which meant that we had it fairly good compared to what she had. I wonder what my nan would have said to the kids of today. Something like this maybe: 'All you kids today are spoilt and it's our fault! We gave you bedrooms like apartments, with handpainted designer wallpaper. The only thing we had on our wall was damp. You get pushed around now in £15,000 prams. We were bounced over the cobbles in a washhouse pram, no wonder we bloody stuttered! And your babies are all dressed up, like, *What Ever Happened to Baby Jane?* We didn't have TK Maxx, Matalan or Primark. No wonder I was an ugly baby, sitting in the pram dressed as a Japanese sniper. And what do you get kids now as a snack? Little tiny pots of yoghurt! We got Phenergan! Phenergan? That's sleep medicine! But yer mam used to feed it to you, spoon after spoon, and then yer nan would come in, rag the dummy out of your mouth, stick it in her whisky and ram it back in. I was stoned out of my brain and couldn't sit up till I was three and a half! And we didn't have baby monitors, nooo! We didn't even have a crib. A drawer, that's where we were stuck, in the bedroom drawer. And if you cried, your mother would come in and shut the bleedin' drawer!

'And you older kids are a disgrace, with your teeth that look like you've just swallowed a tin of Dulux brilliant white gloss! Veneers? We couldn't even spell the bleedin' word on my day! We got our teeth took out just so we could get a husband. If we didn't then no one would marry us in case we got a tooth complaint and they fell into debt, getting it fixed, as it was so expensive to see a dentist! I was only twenty-one when I had my teeth out!

'As for your instant teabags… Tetley? PG tips? Yorkshire Breakfast! Not in my bloody day! Us older generation of women were the ones who invented the teabag out of pure necessity. We used to wrap dried tea leaves in a bit of muslin with a spoon of connie-onnie (condensed milk), tied with a bit of cotton, and then we'd take it down in the caddy to your grandad, who was usually working as a coggy watchman (night watchman) at a factory, and he'd drop the muslin teabag, which was full of proper Mantunna tea, in the hot water. That's how the bleedin' teabag was invented!'

Yeah, I can imagine my nan saying that, and today's kids not believing a single bleedin' word.

Mam, Dad and Nan weren't the only ones back in the day who used to have to try and make a living. If my parents were skint, that meant we had no pocket money for sweets at all. Being the resourceful little tykes we were, we found lots of ways to make up our sweet fund. Collecting wood was always a good earner. The wood came from the wooden crates thrown down off the top of the Armley and Layfield's factory that stood at the back of the tenements. Once a week, for some strange reason, a man would stand on the factory roof and throw down wooden crates with pictures of oranges on them. 'Fuckin' good firewood, dat!' someone would always say, and we'd gather in gangs at the bottom. All the kids used to stand, looking up and shouting at the men on the roof – 'Hey, mate!', 'Down here, mate!', 'Over 'ere, pal!' And as the boxes tumbled, we would squeal and run away to avoid getting clobbered. I swear those factory workers aimed for us sometimes but we didn't care. Once the boxes hit the ground with an almighty crash, there was a big free-for-all and we'd scurry back to grab as much wood as we could.

Sometimes we'd fight with the other gangs to make sure we'd collect enough to make some money. Then we'd tie the bundles up and drag them through the streets to one of the derelict houses, where no one could see us. We'd sit around snapping the big bits of wood, with our feet against the bottom step of the wooden staircase, making them into smaller, more manageable bundles. Sometimes we'd use a half-brick and batter the wood into even smaller pieces, which always filled out the bundles of kindling. It was so much fun and worth every splinter we got in our hands and fingers.

To carry around our wooden bundles, which we would sell for a penny or whatever anyone would give us, we'd send Brian to fetch his stirrey. A stirrey was a go-kart made of wood, which, if you were lucky, had two big wheels at the back and two smaller ones at the front. Brian's stirrey was an integral part of the business and that made him proud – the firewood business was a good one to be in as a kid.

Sometimes people would give us empty milk bottles as payment. They were worth a penny if you returned them to the dairy. We'd also get paid with lemonade bottles. Those were like gold dust: you got three pennies for returning them to the local corner shop, or to the Alpine van – which I'll fill you in on in a minute. Gradually, the stirrey would fill up with bottles as the wooden bundles were sold and, after a trip to the dairy and the corner shop, our pockets were full. Who needed pocket money? We were earning a living! Once we'd received our payment, we could buy our sweets and we would always take a reserved bundle of wood home to our mam.

If it wasn't wood we were carrying, it was coal. We lived by the reller, which was the slang name for the railway on Edge Hill. And this railway used to transport coal. I remember passing the coal yard, coming back from Ninny Lizzy's, and there was a hole in the fence with coal pouring out of it. Free coal, we thought, a gift from God. At the time me and Brian were pushing our Ian in his pram. What did we do? We piled all the coal we could into the pram, with Ian still in it. Every square inch was full and we piled it so high around Ian, all you could see was his little head poking out, his black hands resting on top.

Ian thought it was great fun; he was the centre of attention and even grabbed a piece of coal to see what it tasted like. He was black as the hobs of hell, but we thought Mam and Dad would be so happy with all the free coal we'd brought home for the family, they wouldn't mind. A little carbolic soap and Ian would be as good as new. Of course, Mam didn't see it that way; she ranted like she was a madwoman: 'What the hell have you done to your brother? He looks like a bleedin' tar baby!' Dad, on the other hand, seemed quite pleased and offloaded every piece of coal: 'Next time, make sure you get coke!' he said, smiling. This was because coke burnt a lot better than coal

We used to burn anything on our fire just to keep the place warm. When we'd get up in the morning we'd be like,

'Where's me shoes?' Then you'd find out they'd been burnt on the fire as they were falling to bits anyway. Falling to bits or not, they were your favourite shoes because you could go out and play in them and get them black or muddy and your mam wouldn't give you a crack on the head as they were tatty and falling apart already.

'Where's me shoes?' I'd say.

'Oh, I burnt them last night coz there was no more coal left.'

Back then, we would be taking doors off and hacking them to bits for firewood. And when we weren't ripping bits of the lino up to put over the holes in the soles of our shoes, we'd be sticking it on the fire and almost choking to death from the thick black smoke it would cause. Anything to save money, that was our goal.

When the leccy man used to call we would do one of two things: all hide until he went away, or let him in and act dodgy as hell. Like a police line-up, we would all stand there as he'd take the drawer out of the electric meter and pour out the coins on to the kitchen table. Instead of the shillings he would expect, there would be a load of halfpennies filed down so they fitted in the meter like shillings. Then the fingers would start pointing, of course: at me and Brian. We always used to get the blame for filing the coins, even though we couldn't even reach the drawer, because our parents would be ashamed for fiddling the leccy. As soon as the leccy man left, Mam and Dad would apologise and make us a treat, like a nice big jam butty.

We couldn't spend money on luxuries back then, so having

a bike was out of the question, unless you ended up with one by chance. The bike I ended up with – by chance – was a black three-wheeler. What happened was Grandad found the bike when he was coming back from the pub, and he took it to the police station. Six months later, after no one had claimed it, the police said he could have it. And although I always wanted a Chopper bike, this three-wheeler was boss. Our Brian would pedal it and I'd stand on the back, like Boadicea, fancying meself like I was some kind of flippin' charioteer.

Some years later, Ian got a Chopper bike, the thing I wanted so much. It had been a dream of mine for a long time to have a brand-new gleaming Chopper all to myself. I even had newspaper and catalogue advertisements that I had cut out, all featuring pictures of Chopper bikes, and if I found an ad with a blonde kid sitting on a Chopper, male or female, I would keep that picture under my pillow like a tooth awaiting a tooth fairy. I suppose a Chopper fairy was too much to ask for; either that, or our Brian had been sneaking the picture and placing it under his pillow.

I was happy that Brian was happy with his bike, but I was also a little jealous, which I think is allowed when you see someone – no matter how dear – riding around on your dream. Fair enough, he used to let me ride the bike whenever I asked – that's if he wasn't already heading off somewhere on it with his Chopper-mounted mates.

I remember Brian had a Parka coat, which he cut the fur off the hood, stuck it on a car aerial and then attached to the back of the seat. He did this because everyone was putting fur tails on their bikes. He thought he'd do the same, only with the fur from his good coat. I must admit that his bike looked great with the fur hanging from it, right up to the moment my mam spotted where he'd gotten the fur from, made him sew it back onto his coat, and then grounded him for a week. As well as fur tails, they used to stick lots of car mirrors on the Chopper bikes. The girls had pretty bikes, nearly always coloured pink. Instead of fur tails, their bikes had streamers hanging from the handlebars to make them look cuter, along with a little basket on the front. I can only think that basket was for training girls how to do the shopping in later life!

The girls I hung around with weren't into bikes like me, they liked roller skates. But these weren't like the skates of today, with rollerblade wheels, these roller skates would fit any size foot, because they had a screw on the bottom; a nut you turned to make them bigger or smaller. And you didn't always have the band at the front of the skate that kept it fastened to your foot as they'd usually snap after a while. So you would get a pair of your mam's tights and wrap them around your foot and the skate about ten times so you could go rallying off along the road with your mates. My mam would be shouting, 'Where the hell are me tights?' Dad would shout, 'Wear your other tights!' to which she would reply, 'The others aren't American Tan!' Mam would only ever wear American Tan coloured tights. Once, when she sent me to buy more, I came home with 'Sand' instead.

'Do they look like American Tan?' she said.

'Yeah, they do.'

Mam gave me a clip around the ear: 'Get them back, and tell Ali you want American Tan!'

I mentioned receiving bottles as payment for the bundles of wood we used to sell as kindling. Well, those bottles were from my favourite vehicle ever, the Alpine van! The Alpine Soft Drinks van is always worthy of a mention in any book or conversation about sixties and seventies Liverpool. For all the poverty there was in the city at that time, and no matter how poor your parents, every family bought fizzy drinks off the Alpine van man. And fizzy drinks were top shelf on the list of things that made a kid's life great. Sweets, crisps, chocolate, fizzy drinks…everything else was either on the second, third, or one of the lower, not worth a fuckin' mention, shelves.

Once a week, on a Thursday late-afternoon, the Alpine van man would pull into the tenements in his huge, open-backed wagon, carrying hundreds of bottles of our favourite drinks. Mam and Dad never called him the Alpine man; to them and to us kids, he was affectionately known as 'Mr Fizzy Pop'. He didn't have music playing, like the ice cream or the candy floss van. Nah, Mr Fizzy Pop didn't go in for all that bravado, he had a plain wagon with a rusted chain to stop his crates falling off the back. The Alpine drinks came in lots of different flavours, including Dandelion & Burdock, American Cream Soda, Pineapple, Cola, Limeade, Orangeade, Cherryade, Lemonade, Shandy and Gingerade.

In our house we used to buy six bottles a week: three Dandelion & Burdock and three American Cream Soda. We chose these flavours because they seemed more exotic than the others and each had another function besides being a tasty drink: when ice cream was added to the cream soda, it made the perfect ice cream float, and when frozen on a stick, no other flavour came near to the Dandelion & Burdock lolly-ice.

I remember looking forward to Thursdays at about 4.30 p.m. when Mr Fizzy Pop would pull into view. I also remember when he refused to sell us any more drinks because we'd stopped returning the bottles. Everyone returned the Alpine bottles because you got money back when you did. Not my dad. He decided that the bottles – which were made of super-thick glass – would be the perfect bottles to hold his home-brewed bitter and beer in. It didn't take long for Mr Fizzy Pop to suss out that our family was the only one buying, but not returning, the bottles. So in the end we were excluded from the pop run and had to reach out to our next-door neighbour to buy fizzy pop for us.

No prizes for guessing that the next-door neighbour stopped buying our drinks when Mr Fizzy Pop complained that she wasn't returning the right amount of bottles. So, after a while, my mam clamped down on my dad using the bottles for his home brew, and after an apology to Mr Fizzy Pop, things went back to normal. By this time Dad had a hoard of Alpine bottles that he, Uncle Freddie (Dad's brother) and Uncle Tommy (Dad's brother-in-law) had collected. And yes, Uncle Freddie and Uncle Tommy had also been reprimanded by Mr Fizzy Pop for not returning bottles at their houses.

Mam always accused the three of them of watching far too

much telly: 'Been watching *The Dukes of Hazzard* again, have you?' she'd say, shaking her head as they messed around with their vile-smelling concoction. 'Or is it a "recipe" from *The Waltons*?' She was, of course, referring to the illegal moonshine whisky featured at one time or another in both of these TV shows. 'You won't be saying that when you're knocking them back and having a dance, Margie,' my dad would say, smiling as Mam sighed and rolled her eyes.

I remember the day Dad and Uncle Freddie and Uncle Tommy first brought the beer-making stock home. I swear they thought they were gonna be the next Cains Brewery. However, they only had some tubes, a bucket and a load of yeast. The first batch failed miserably, but Dad and both my uncles still drank what they'd made and were sick for a week. The second batch was slightly better, but didn't have any flavour and was so strong all three of them were found passed out next to the still. The third batch was inspired by something Uncle Tommy had seen in a magazine about wine making. He suggested to Dad and Freddie that they add rhubarb for flavour, failing to tell them this was best used for wine making. They all loved the flavour, but it gave them and all of their mates the shits.

The leftover bottles of rhubarb beer were placed in the cupboard next to the hot water tank. Back then, the tank didn't have lagging and so the rhubarb beer fermented, expanded and heated up until… Bang! We all shit ourselves…Bang! We thought a bomb had gone off… Bang!

Mam looked at my dad and shook her head. The cupboard was destroyed, with broken glass sticking out everywhere.

Four different neighbours came banging on our door to see if we were being attacked or had found an unexploded bomb or something. One neighbour woke her son up and sent him off to get the police in case we needed help. Me and our Brian were jumping all over the place, fully wired, as Dad had made us finish off two Dandelion & Burdocks so he could use the bottles for his beer. After that the family brewery base of operations was relocated to Uncle Tommy's shed.

CHAPTER TWENTY-SEVEN

CHRIMBO

Woolworths department store was a great place to be at Christmas time. In fact, all of the old department stores were a hive of free entertainment at Christmas. Blacklers department store was even better as it had a Christmas bargain basement that seemed to go on for miles, where you could buy absolutely anything you could think of for the cheapest ever prices. When you went up to the first floor in Blacklers, you could have a ride on the oversized rocking horse, but there was always a security guard who'd shout, 'Gerroff! You've been on it long enough!' However, when the same security guard saw you with your mam he'd be all nice and sweet, and let you stay on for as long as you liked, which wasn't long, as my mam would have less patience than him and rag me off after ten seconds.

Whenever I came to town with Mam, whether it was Christmas time or summer, I used to get a clip round my head when the bus turned the corner by Lewis's department store, because halfway up the building, on eye-level to the upper deck of the bus, there stood the statue of a naked man. It was known affectionately as 'Dickie Lewis' for obvious reasons really. The naked man was a sailor looking out to sea, but why the hell he was in the raw always puzzled me and everyone else who saw him. Did sailors often strip off in the old days and go hanging out on buildings in the buff? Anyhow, if ever I was on the bus with my mam or Nan, and got caught having a quick blimp of a bronze willy, I'd expect to get a clip round my ear, followed by the immortal words, 'Don't be looking at that, it'll poke your eyes out!'

Lewis's department store came into its own at Christmas time, when the store would decorate their windows for the Christmas grotto – or 'Santa's grotto' as we called it. I remember at that time there weren't very many shiny, colourful things to see – the colour and shine came later when glam rock invaded our TV screens. But the windows of Lewis's brought colour and shininess to all our lives. However, they always put paper coverings across the windows until it was time for the big reveal. I'd be at one end of the window, trying to see if there was a gap in the paper covering big enough to spot the shiny Christmas stuff behind.

'Can you see anything?' I'd shout to me mates, who were lying on the pavement, cricking their necks to try and see around the paper.

'No,' they'd say, 'he's done it up impossible again!' Which meant the guy with the paper and sticky tape had done his job well – the bloody jobsworth!

Finally, they would unveil the window to crowds of shoppers, three hundred deep and causing all the traffic to stop as they stood in the road. The crowd always gasped and then cheered as they were treated to the most magical thing you could ever imagine as a child. The window was shining, with coloured tinsel and a tree decked in lights and decorations, and the most beautiful baubles in glitter, or crystal-clear. Some of the larger baubles had figures inside: Santa, reindeers, elves and Christmas trees. The floor of the window was covered in cotton wool, which had been sprinkled with a shimmering layer of silver glitter. And taking pride of place in the main window was the huge Christmas tree that was covered from base to tip with every decoration a child could fantasise about. At the top of the tree was either an angel or a shining star.

After standing in awe and pointing out our favourite bits of the window display, me and my friends would almost jump up and down in anticipation of seeing the next part of the Lewis's Christmas experience – the arrival of Santa himself. We would almost pee ourselves with excitement as we heard the crowds near St George's Hall start screaming, cheering and then clapping as the large float carrying Santa and his reindeer passed by on his way to us. And each part of the city centre he passed, the crowds in that part also screamed, cheered and clapped. If you could compare those sounds of joy to anything, you might say it was like an audible Mexican wave slowly heading towards you.

Then, at last, the sound grew so loud we knew Santa was here, and we – like those thousands of people before us –

continued the audible wave by screaming, cheering and then clapping till our little hands were red. The huge float was like its own personal carnival. It was decked with a zillion decorations made to look like a snowy scene in Lapland or somewhere you were guaranteed lovely soft clean snow, not the mud-grey slush we usually stuck with. The centre part of the float had Santa's sleigh and his large reindeer, which were made from plastic, but to us they looked real enough to eat the carrots some soft sod in the crowd threw at them.

In the seat sat Santa himself, with his curly flowing white beard and red velvet clothes. And he had a speaker too, because he was a modern Santa, with all the latest Santa tech, and all you could hear was, 'Ho, ho, ho, merry Christmas!' The whole crowd shouted 'Merry Christmas' back in the most Scally Scouse voices ever. I remember eagerly waving at Santa and, for a second, he looked at me and waved back. That little experience, just a second long glance, really made my memories of that time even more magical.

Another brilliant thing about the float was Santa's helpers – elves that ran up and down the float, throwing sweets into the crowd. Talk about a Royal Rumble! As the sweets came flying, me and me mates turned into quarterbacks and battled our way up, down, through and along the crowd, snatching as many sweets as we could. You see, back then, getting sweets thrown to you was like Charlie Bucket finding a Wonka Golden Ticket – rare as hens' teeth. You truly took a chance of being trampled to death for the sake of a Mojo.

Although we saw Santa and his elves and reindeer, and we got lots of sweets and were amazed and enchanted by the displays in Lewis's window, we were always a little sad that we couldn't afford to see Santa's Grotto inside the department store. This grotto was the best in the city. Instead, Mam would take us to TJ Hughes's on London Road, which wasn't as good, but we always loved it when we got there. Besides, TJ's had the Dancing Waters, a kind of leaping water display – they call them 'sprinklers' nowadays – but these sprinklers were synchronised to music. I swear the synchronised water outside the Balagio in Las Vegas stole their idea from TJ Hughes. Inside TJ's store, we got to see a much cheaper-looking Santa, whose beard wasn't curly at all. He'd give each of us either a present wrapped in pink tissue paper, or one wrapped in blue tissue. Our Brian got one of those cheap plastic guns that you put caps in, but Mam said, 'You're not getting any caps for that!' So Brian made more noise pretending the gun was firing than he ever could have made with the caps. I got one of those dolls that didn't move any of its limbs; it was just plastic without any bleedin' detail at all. It didn't even have clothes on, or nothing.

Armed with our freebie presents, we'd march back into town to watch the Christmas lights being switched on. Standing there freezing to death, all staring up at the huge Christmas tree that had travelled from Switzerland or Lapland (or somewhere else with 'land' in its name). Then the countdown began: ten, nine…one, the lights went on! Everyone cheered and then fell silent, taking in the sparkle of the Christmas lights. Sometimes I wish those events had been frozen in time, just like our fingers and toes were in the snow.

Christmas was different for everyone back then. We all knew that Santa Claus provided all our presents, so we poorer kids couldn't quite understand how the well-off kids, whose parents could afford to buy them presents themselves had they chosen to do so, always seemed to get more and better presents than other kids whose parents were living on the breadline. I mean, you'd think the fat git would have been able to even it out a little better, wouldn't you? Our Christmases were not fancy – they were basic, with only one or two little presents and a bag or two of sweets each. But to us they were special and not once did we ever wake up disappointed.

We always wished for one thing that we never saw on Christmas Day: snow. No matter how hard we wanted to see those soft little white flakes falling past our window as we opened our presents, they never did. It was snowing in Ireland, Scotland – all the bloody time in Scotland – and even in Wales. They all had white Christmases, but in dreary old England, we never did. Yet on the TV they always showed these oldie-worldy festive films that had England looking like it was friggin' Lapland or the North Pole.

Ebenezer Scrooge was always shown walking to work at Scrooge & Marley on Christmas Day, knee-deep in snow. It turns out the reason Charles Dickens set lots of his stories on snowy Christmas days was because as a kid, the lucky little bastard spent six of his first nine Christmases playing snowballs on Christmas morning, and there have been only seven white Christmases since… Bah – fuckin' – humbug! Luckily, every now and then it would snow close enough to Christmas to make us all feel festive. And when it did, no matter what we were supposed to be doing – work, chores, dying of cholera, whatever – we would drop everything, wrap up as warm as possible and head out into the whiteness. Usually we would just play in the courtyard with the other kids, but the snow was already disturbed and snowmen were everywhere. So, sometimes Brian, Ian and me would go off like three little Scotts of the Antarctic to the cathedral graveyard and spend the day playing there amongst the undisturbed snow. It was like a white blanket coating everything, and I remember me, Ian and our Brian pausing for what seemed like forever, just taking in the Christmas postcard scene that stretched out before us. Added to that, the gravestones made the whole thing look like a Christmas ghost story, even though it was daytime. Then we would run – well, stamp – our way through the snow, leaving the first footprints that spiralled around the whole of the graveyard. After disturbing as much snow as possible we would pelt each other with snowballs and then attempt to build a giant snowman. We used to spend ages rolling up a gigantic ball of snow for the body, but by the time that was accomplished we were so tired out, the rest of the body and head were tiny in comparison. Like all kids, we dreaded when the lovely crisp snow turned into the inevitable slush, though it still didn't stop us from chucking slush balls.

Afterwards we would head for home bloody freezing, our toes throbbing and our legs ripped to bits with welly rash. All three of us would jostle for position, trying to hog the roaring fire to get warm, until our skin turned bright red, causing Nan to say, 'Don't be standing too close to the bloody fire. You'll get corned-beef legs!' We would keep those snowy memories locked firmly in our minds for a month or more until Christmas came, believing this would somehow bring more snowfall on Christmas Day, but, as I said before, it never did.

I think the best Christmas I ever had, even to this day, was Christmas 1966, when I was eight years old. That year Santa was particularly generous and it was such a coincidence – to us kids, anyway – that in that particular year our mam and dad could have afforded to buy our presents without any help from Santa whatsoever. I remember that Christmas so well because we all got a World Cup Willie mascot to celebrate the fact that England had kicked the Germans' butt and won the World Cup that summer, and Dad had been knocked over by a wagon some months earlier while delivering parcels for the railway (he worked on the railway, delivering parcels).

But my mam used to always think that he wasn't going to work, for some strange reason. So she used to say to us, 'You're not going to school today.' And we were like, 'Aw, not again, Mam!' and she'd make us hide in the back of the van when Dad was going to work so we could spy and see if he really was going to work or skiving. He'd easily spot us and shout, 'What are you doing in here?' Then he'd have to drop us off at school late and he'd be late for work. But we wouldn't want to grass on Mam, so we would just pretend we wanted to ride around with him – that way he was far too confused to hit us.

Dad had been run over because he saw our Brian crossing

the road into traffic and he pushed him out of the way and got hit by the car himself. Thankfully, he wasn't too badly hurt, but he was awarded £100 compensation in the middle of December 1966. I swear he spent every penny of it on that Christmas. Mam could hardly contain herself; she had woken us at five in the morning to show us how good Santa had been, but I'd been awake earlier than that as I could smell the Christmas dinner being prepared. Mam was wide awake and grinning like a Cheshire cat as us bleary-eyed youngsters were shook from our slumber and ushered to the bottom of the bed.

That year, we were absolutely loaded with presents. We started with the pillowcases by the bottom of the bed: cars, a Snakes and Ladders board game, Tiddlywinks and a climb-in *Dr Who* Dalek for Ian. In the living room, there were two dolls for me – a Tiny Tears and a Tressy – and in the middle of the room was a large police car with a siren, a Spirograph, KerPlunk, lots of stocking-filler toys and chocolate too.

I can't recall what Mam and Dad bought for each other as I was too engrossed in unwrapping my own pressies. Other presents we opened held lovely warm jumpers and pullovers and we got a pair of gloves each. After breakfast we went out and played with our toys. Afterwards, we met up with friends and all played together in the tenement courtyard. Then, when our mams started calling us in for our Christmas dinners, we shouted, 'Coming!' and ran our separate ways without even acknowledging each other.

Now, we loved Christmas dinner even at our poorest

times. At these times our presents were wrapped in the *Echo* newspaper and Christmas dinner was a small chicken. But in 1966, we had a dinner to remember. Crispy potatoes, gammon, chicken, sprouts, Bisto gravy mixed with the fat off the chicken and the gammon, and all the other trimmings that I shovelled into my mouth without knowing what they were. After dinner, we were to let our food settle for a good half hour before moving on to the afters, but Dad suddenly leapt up and shouted, 'Trifle time!' We all leapt up too, shouting the same thing repeatedly. Mam just rolled her eyes and said, 'Oh, go on then. It is Christmas.' I have never seen a large trifle disappear so quickly. It was gorgeous, the most wonderful thing I had ever tasted, except for Mam's gravy, that is. She had made the trifle from scratch an' all. It wasn't one of those shop-bought things. There was fresh fruit and cream and it had grated walnuts too, with grated lemon and orange zest.

I'm describing that Christmas Day as clearly as it still is in my mind. My mam suffered with nerves every other day of the year except that day. She and Dad sat together, looking contented and happy, filled to the brim with Christmas food and drink. Nan insisted on cleaning every plate, bowl, knife, fork and spoon as soon as it was used, which was her way of having a happy Christmas. Me, Brian and Ian just played to our heart's content – it really was a wonderful day.

CHAPTER TWENTY-EIGHT

SCHOOL HELL

The less I say about school, the better, although I find myself having to add something about my school years, if only to fill in the multiples of five days a week where my whereabouts need to be accounted for. School was never a good thing with me, but here goes...

Our primary school was St Saviour's, which was located close to home on Crown Street. Most of the family went there, including Dad and my aunties and uncles. My form, or class teacher, Mr Lewis, had a mouth like a foghorn and the weirdest and bushiest eyebrows you could ever see, the kind of eyebrows the girls stick on their faces nowadays. Mr Lewis was a prick; a bad teacher, pure and simple. He loved making my schooldays into a living hell. Bad teachers are usually the type that are either pissed off with the job, or near to retirement; teachers who have become jaded by the kids who have helped turn what was once their teaching dream into the career from hell. These 'bad' teachers never seem to direct their anger at the kids who deserve it, they always look for that kid in the classroom that they can bully. Well, I was that kid.

'Murray, I can't believe how thick you are! You're as thick as a brick!' This is what I heard almost every day in Mr Lewis's class. 'Thicklet!' he'd say, and the kids – who are, after all, only kids – would laugh their heads off and point at me, or agree with their prick of a teacher. Mr Lewis kept up his barrage of insults throughout the school terms, constantly calling me 'thick' and 'idiot' and the kids kept laughing. I started that school with a lot more friends than when I finished it – after all, what kid wants to hang around with the kid with a teacher's target on their back? The teacher might then turn their attention to you. So, my friends were mostly from the other classes.

Mr Lewis would make me his whipping boy (or girl) whenever his class wasn't doing that well in the school class ratings. 'I wonder why our class is third this year, Murray,' he'd say, all snide and horrible like. 'Could it be because the other two classes haven't got a thick idiot ruining their average score?'

So, after years of crap off a teacher who was in fact bullying me on a daily basis, I decided to hit back. So, I made a stand: I gave up on learning and I was done with his abuse. I started playing up in class, talking when he was talking, laughing with the other kids at anything Lewis said. When he asked me a question I knew the answer to, I would deliberately give the wrong answer. He would glare at me and say, 'Murray, you really are as thick as two short planks, aren't you?' 'Yeah, what else is new?' I would say. His abusive words soon became water off a duck's back.

Then one day we got to watch a film in class that was all about how deserts are formed. I was engrossed because it was so interesting, seeing other parts of the world. Then the film was over and the lights came on, and Mr Lewis decided to target me once again.

'What was the film called, Murray?'

'I don't know sir.' I replied, and this time I truly didn't know the answer.

Mr Lewis kicked off at me, but this time I gave as good as I got and found myself standing outside the classroom, staring down the corridor. That day Mr Lewis gave me the cane and he hit as hard as a grown man could. I could never understand that, and I wondered why a person who is supposed to enlighten and educate a child so that they are prepared for life as an adult would want to hurt a child who has never wronged them. All I learnt from that pathetic man was that I was thick, and I couldn't read because I was thick, and his class performed badly because I was a part of it. I should have told my mam or dad, or even my nan about him and his bullying ways 'cause any one of them would have flown up to the school and beaten the crap out of him, but we didn't know we were supposed to report bullying teachers back then; they were adults and we thought that them bullying us was just part of life and what you had to go through when you were a kid.

At the age of eleven I finally got to say goodbye to St

Saviour's and started my new school, Paddy Comp (Paddington Comprehensive). I'd been looking forward to going, but at the same time I was a little scared as I had heard that they put the new kids through extreme initiation ceremonies. I remember the day I got my first school uniform that was bought with a grant. Like the Queen of the Catwalk, I was walking up and down in front of my mam and dad, while Mam pulled at the skirt and blazer to make sure they fitted perfectly. I just pranced and pirouetted around with a huge smile on my face.

My St Saviour's education hadn't prepared me for secondary school, as I discovered on my first day at Paddy. Day one, we were given a map on arrival, which had all of our classes for the day and directions on how to get to each class. The school was absolutely huge and overbearing at first, especially as I couldn't read most of the directions – thank you, Mr Lewis! – I looked like a tourist wandering the corridors, asking directions. I was put in class G11, which was Progress Class, the class for no-hopers, who weren't progressing at all. Dunces, the hard of thinking... Generally, the kids as thick as two short planks were placed in this class and ignored for most of the time.

There was always the odd teacher who would invest time in trying to teach us Progressive kids, but most gave up before they started. Our PE (Physical Education) teacher, Mr Clark, was one of the many teachers who really didn't think those kids in Progressive Class were worth the effort. As soon as we'd show up for our PE lesson, he would have beanbags already placed around the gymnasium floor.

'Pick a beanbag, get into twos and throw the bags to each other!'

And that was it, half an hour throwing beanbags at each other while Clark sat reading the paper.

I remember the only day he showed any interest was when he had us watch a programme on the Olympic Games, showing the long jumper, Bob Beamon, winning his Olympic gold medal for a world record jump that stood for 23 years. It was the first and only time I ever saw Mr Clark passionate about anything. I remember him saying, 'Could you imagine 29 foot two and a quarter inches? They didn't even have an implement long enough to measure the jump.' He then produced a tape measure of his own and measured the exact distance out on the gym mats, and for that half hour, we all tried leaping as far as we could just to see how impossible a thing Bob Beamon had achieved.

Mr Clark was a different person that day, and the little bit of attention given to us made us kids different too.

Our lessons in Paddy Comp were more difficult than they had been in St Saviour's, but because they weren't headed by Mr Lewis, they didn't seem all that bad. I remember we had a chemistry teacher who liked to think of himself as abusive and bullying, but compared to the prick Mr Lewis he was a bunny rabbit. At least he was until the day Susan Haygan wondered what it would be like to shove a Bunsen burner up her nostril and turn it on. She smiled at me and the rest of the transfixed class with such a satisfied smile I actually considered doing the same thing. Then she hit the deck: lights out, smack on the floor, unconscious. As she lay panting on the floor, the Bunsen tube still hanging from her nostril, the chemistry teacher went apeshit. You could tell he was in two minds whether to kick her or resuscitate her; he decided on the latter by throwing a cup of ice-cold water in her face. When I think back on the events of that day I'm shocked that we all took it with a pinch of salt. It didn't faze us, and we laughed about it for weeks. Nobody got into trouble and life went on. Nowadays the chemistry teacher would be sacked and maybe even locked up.

As well as being in the Progressive Class and being looked down on by other students, some of us were also singled out because our parents didn't have any money. Discrimination was a big thing back then; anything to pick on those kids who didn't automatically fit the school profile. Me and a small group of other kids topped the list of the discriminated: we were the poor and progressive, we had free school dinner tickets and anything else that was free. I have to admit the school dinner tickets were great because we could sell them to fat kids with money, go out of a lunch time and get up to no good. But when the time came around for the school photos, being poor really put you in the limelight. All of the kids in your year would line up to get their photos taken, but then the teacher would walk along and single out the poor kids from the line and send them back to their class. I once asked a particularly nasty teacher why he was taking me out of the line: 'What's the point of keeping you in the photos if your dad can't afford to buy them?' he said. What a bastard, to say that in front of everyone! I think it was the one time in Paddy when I had flashbacks of Mr Lewis. Luckily, I didn't have this prick for any of my lessons so I resisted the urge to mouth off and call him all the fuck-face bastards in the world.

Most of my school life at Paddy Comp was spent outside its gates. I figured, why bother going in when nobody is really interested in teaching me? By law, they had to have me in the school and had to be seen to be giving me some sort of education, but the only thing I really learnt was a number of ways to play truant. In those days I got most of my education from hanging around the town centre and the city's many parks. I'd given up on education because education had long ago given up on me. If I was ever to find a way in life, then it would be under my own steam and my own understanding of how this world functions, its challenges, and how to meet those bastards head-on.

CHAPTER TWENTY-NINE

BOYFRIENDS?

Welcome to the shortest chapter in the entire fuckin' book! As a kid, I never really had a boyfriend because I was such a tomboy. My mates were all nice-looking – well, they were better-looking than me. My hair was like rats' tails. I remember I liked this lad called Craig, and I used to practise kissing him on the back of my hand. I'd say to myself if I was gonna kiss him, I'd kiss him like this: mmmmmwah! So, my first boyfriend was the back of my hand... Talk about leading a sheltered life!

My second boyfriend – which only confirms my leading a sheltered life – was Troy Tempest, a bleedin' puppet from the kids' TV show, *Stingray*. I absolutely adored Troy, and the back of my hand got lots of kissing action whenever I thought of him. The lead pilot of the underwater craft *Stingray*, he was always out for risking his life to save the planet from baddies. I was absolutely mortified when I first found out he was a puppet, although I always wondered why he walked so funny. I remember I even learnt to swim because I wanted to be like Troy's love interest, Marina – it didn't matter that she didn't talk because she was so gorgeous-looking – slightly blank-faced maybe – but gorgeous all the same; especially to me.

My other fave TV shows were *Thunderbirds* and *Fireball XL5*, and when *Joe 90* came along, he made it cool for kids to wear glasses. Michael Caine had made wearing specs cool for adults, and Joe had done the same for us kids – although, once again, he was only a puppet – Joe 90, I mean, not Michael Caine. Even the kids with a plaster over the bridge of their glasses suddenly looked cool, and if they weren't like Joe 90, they were compared to the Milky Bar Kid from the TV adverts – which wasn't quite so cool, but he did have a gun. Then someone started the term 'four-eyes' and everyone would say to the kids with glasses, 'Shurrup, Four-eyes!' All of a sudden, wearing glasses was very un-cool. It's funny how trends change, because back then if you had braces on your teeth, they used to call you 'girder-gob'. Now, if you have braces they're considered fashionable and teenagers (and a number of trendy adults) actually want braces so they can look cool.

So, what has all that got to do with boyfriends? Well, I did say my experience with boyfriends was non-existent, so I had to throw that stuff in to pad out the chapter… Sorry!

CHAPTER THIRTY

FAME AT LAST!

'You've got big dreams. You want fame. Well, fame costs. And right here is where you start paying: in sweat' – Lydia Grant, *Fame*

Now, some – hopefully all – of you reading my joys and woes will know of my acting career and will have hopefully followed it at some stage. But how it all started was a very odd thing indeed. Would you believe I used to be a Diddy Man? I was one of Ken Dodd's Diddy Men! The first time I heard them mentioned in our house was when my dad spotted something in the *Liverpool Echo* newspaper. Dad said that the famous comedian Ken Dodd was holding auditions in Liverpool to find some more Diddy Men for his show. Now, at that time I was an avid watcher of Ken Dodd and his Diddy Men, who weren't really men, but little kids dressed up as midgets. I used to watch them on a Sunday morning and sing along to all of their songs.

'You should go for that, our Christine,' said Dad. I thought he was being funny as he'd seen me dance and heard me sing and therefore knew that I was no good at either. As I lay awake in bed that night, I started having dreams of grandeur, of fame and superstardom. The memories of dancing around in our hallway with an audience made up of old coats came flooding back to me. *What's the worst that can happen? If I go along and I don't get picked, I might still get to meet Ken Dodd, and he would be the first famous person I'd met*, I thought to myself.

So, I talked myself into it, and the following Saturday, after practising a song for the audition, my mam gave me a bottle of water and the bus fare into town. I remember sitting on the bus singing, 'My Boy Lollipop', a favourite song of mine by the singer Millie Small. I'd asked the bus driver if he could give me a shout when it was my stop and, thankfully, he did, because I was in full rehearsal haze.

I arrived on the opposite side from the Royal Court theatre and swallowed hard as I looked at the humongous queue that stretched all the way around the block. The queue was full of privileged theatre school kids, with their crazy mothers pushing them to get their songs right and telling them how they should smile at Mr Dodd. They reminded me of the pushy parents described in the book, *Charlie and the Chocolate Factory*. At that point I really thought that I didn't have the slightest chance in hell of landing a Diddy Man part, as I knew, after hearing some of the kids' singing voices, that I was nowhere near their league. But I had attitude, and so I forced myself into the queue right near the front. I kept my eyes facing forward for I knew that if I looked back, my gaze would be met by hundreds of angry hopefuls and their parents, pissed off with me for pushing in!

It was just as well I did push in near the front, as a man suddenly appeared from inside the theatre and told the hundreds of kids behind me that they wouldn't be getting in. As you can imagine, there was a breakout of crying, snotty noses and cursing parents. Me and around one hundred other kids were ushered into the theatre and then split into groups of twelve. The group of kids I hooked up with were all dressed up and looked really professional. After a while, we were called forward by a lady with white hair and told to go to the back of the stage. At the front of the stage a woman sat at a table, taking names. I pushed to the front.

'Name?' the lady asked.

'Christine Murray.'

'Age?'

'Eleven.'

Then she asked me what was the name of my dance school, and with that one question, all of my hopes and dreams shattered. I said nothing. The lady looked up.

'You are with a dance school?'

Dad had said sod all about having to have attended a dance school. I didn't know any dance school names so I wasn't even able to blag that I'd been to one. St Saviour's was on the tip of my tongue when I heard a voice from behind me say, 'What have I told you about wandering off?'

The lady whose voice I'd heard walked up to me and placed her hand on my shoulder. She looked at the lady at the table and announced, 'She's with the Vera Corrine Dancing School.' Then she smiled and winked at me. The lady at the table asked what I was going to sing.

'"My Boy Lollipop" by Millie Small,' I said, almost shouting.

And so I sang while accompanied by a man on a piano. And as I sang, I once again remembered singing and dancing with the coats in our hallway, where I imagined I was someone famous like Lucille Ball. Now, it was for real, and I stood a chance of achieving my dreams. So, I sang with all of my heart, like I was performing as Annie on the West End stage.

When the song ended, there was a deathly silence. I'd always expected if you gave a good singing performance, people would give a round of applause, but I couldn't hear anything. Was my singing that bad? I later found out that people don't applaud auditions. Vera Corrine took me to one side: 'So, little miss,' she whispered, 'you fancy yourself as a performer then?'

I shrugged my shoulders and told her I liked Pan's People on *Top of the Pops*. Vera laughed her head off and then told me that she had seen a certain look in my eye when I walked on to the stage, that's why she'd stepped forward. She said I had a look of eagerness and excitement and it showed when I sang my audition song. She then said that the lady at the desk had also noticed the same thing.

'So, what's your name again?'

'It's Christine, miss.'

'Well, Christine, mine's Vera, but the girls call me Auntie Vera.'

And then she went on to say the nicest words I had ever heard:

'Christine, would you like to join my dancing school?'

I was speechless, and it was the first time I had ever felt lightheaded enough to faint. All I could do was nod eagerly. I remember later that day telling my family about the day's events and all of us dancing around as I sang 'My Boy Lollipop' over and over. And everyone was proud of me. Me! I could just see it in their faces. And them being proud was as alien to me as it was to my parents, for up to that moment there had never been an occasion where I'd made them proud. But in my defence, most kids don't make their parents proud until they grow up and build a well in Africa or something.

The following Saturday, I joined Vera's dance school in the Dingle area of the city. Everyone there had a basic knowledge of dance and one or two were really amazing dancers. I was in awe as I watched them practising their dance moves: some did tap, others did ballet. Then we heard that three of Vera Corrine's dancers had been chosen to be in Ken Dodd's Diddy Men. For a moment I felt sad, as I'd forgotten that I was auditioned as part of the school, but when I remembered, the excitement was palpable, electric and unlike anything I'd felt before. There were at least forty-five hopeful girls, all talented, so the odds of ragamuffin Crissy getting a place? Well, let's just say the odds were not in my favour, but I was still excited and, what's more, I had hope.

Two girls' names were read out, one after the other, and both times the room went insane, everybody trying to hug the girls all at the same time. And then it was time to announce the final winner, the lucky girl who had landed the final Diddy Man part and would go on to meet Ken Dodd and be in his show, singing and dancing and earning a wage too. 'And the third successful auditionee is… Christine Murray!'

I nearly shat myself. For a moment I thought, *what are the friggin' odds of two Christine Murrays both attending the same dance school?* Then I realised it was me, my name, just me! Needless to say, there were celebrations in the Murray household that day. And so I was one of Ken Dodd's Diddy Men.

I was at Vera Corrine's school of dancing for almost two years and she really did earn the nickname 'Auntie' as she was a warm and lovely person, who genuinely cared about the wellbeing of the girls that she taught, and she loved every one of us like we were her daughters.

Thank you so much, Vera.

CHAPTER THIRTY-ONE

NAN

Now, there is no single chapter in this book dedicated to my mam or dad, who I love with all my heart, and some of you might be asking, 'Hey, Crissy, why have you written a whole chapter about your nan and not your mam an' dad?' The answer to that can be put in a number of ways, but I prefer this one: As a kid, you are far less likely to swear in front of nephews and nieces than your brothers and sisters. The reason for this is you're stuck with your siblings (and most of the time they're doing your fuckin' noggin in), while your nephews and nieces can go home to their own houses.

Do you see what I mean? No? Okay, I'll put it this way: Nephews and nieces are around you because they choose to be, otherwise they would just not bother. The same with your nan – she doesn't have to be there for you, you're not her kid, and she isn't your parent. Therefore, she has chosen to be around you and look after you and put the time into making sure you're okay, fed and happy, even though that's not her job. And so, the reason I have a chapter dedicated to Nan, besides loving the very bones of her, is because she chose to be there for me every day without her presence being her duty or a foregone conclusion.

Henrietta, or Hetty, as everyone called her, was my mam's mam, and my nan. She wasn't too tall, only five foot in stockinged feet, with long, fair hair, and was like a little pocket rocket, running here and there, always on the go from the moment she woke up till she went to bed. I was always a little bit amazed as to how she managed to keep going without any complaint or gripe. You would never hear Nan moaning about work or everyday chores. In fact, she was the opposite. The only sound you did hear her make while working was her singing: Nan loved to sing. Most of the songs I know from back then weren't the ones I listened to on Nan's radiogram, they're the ones I heard her singing as she was dusting, polishing or washing the house and us.

As well as her constant singing, which could cheer anyone out of even the deepest doldrums, my nan had a brilliant sense of humour and would constantly make anyone she was around laugh their heads off. I like to think that I inherited her sense of humour, although she would never have come out with the type of jokes that I do in my act, she'd have probably given me a clip around the ear on my first swear word. Her skin was like silk because she always used Johnson's Baby Lotion, but her hands were rough as dockers' hands and I don't think she had fingerprints as she'd Vim'd them off with all the scrubbing she did.

Nan never really had much of anything her whole life. As a young girl, she – and a lot of young women at that time – had every one of her teeth taken out. The reason for this horrible practice was all down to attracting a husband. If a woman had her own teeth then, sooner or later, tooth decay would start mounting up dental bills and the married couple would fall into debt, etc. So, as a preventative to debt and ruin, the young women sacrificed their natural smiles. This would usually take place when she got married, and – as a wedding present – a new set of dentures was made to replace her teeth. This was practiced all over the country.

I'll always remember she had a lone gold tooth set in her false teeth, which glistened like a star in the world's warmest smile. As well as the gold tooth, Nan had a thin wedding band and that was all the possessions she needed. My Nan ran the cleanest household of any woman then and any woman I have met since then. The windows in our flat were spotless. If I pressed my face to the window and left a smudge, you could bet your life that sometime within an hour, that window would be polished and pristine. The step outside our house practically gleamed, no matter how many times it was stood on. It was this way because Nan cleaned it at least three times a week with 'Vim' and, once scoured, she would even sand the stone a little to make an edge more perfect than any of the steps belonging to our neighbours.

It really was a wonder how that step was still there after

all the years of washing, scrubbing and sanding it endured. To look at Nan's perfect shiny step from the landing of the tenement block where we lived, you'd think we lived in a palace – either that, or we were expecting a royal visit! But all of this was an illusion, a stage backdrop painted to fool the audience, the outside world.

Nan worked as cleaner in our school, St Saviour's. She was in there throughout the week, from the early hours and during the day. It was very hard work and most of it consisted of being on your hands and knees scrubbing floors, but you would never hear my nan complain: it was work, and she was glad to have the work.

When she was young, Nan worked for Bryant & May, the company that made safety matches. Now, Bryant & May had a huge match factory in Speke, Merseyside. Working at the factory was about the most dangerous job you could do and akin to working in one of those factories in World War II, the ones that made the explosive shells. At any moment the whole of Bryant & May could combust, like any of the matches they manufactured, and burn to the ground in minutes. But my nan didn't ever dwell on that fact when reminiscing about her time working there. She only ever mentioned that she had lots of friends at that factory and she spent a lot of time swimming when she worked there.

Friggin' strange or what, working with matches while swimming? Well, it wasn't that strange. Nan was an excellent swimmer – in fact, she was so good, the Bryant & May company asked her to swim for their Speke branch in the annual swimming competitions they used to have against other companies in the area. As Nan loved swimming, she immediately said yes, and started kicking ass. She actually won lots of times, and she won lots of prizes, prizes I wish we still had to this day. Unfortunately, at that time, with money being in short supply, she would very often have to pawn the prizes and as they weren't considered essentials, they would be left in the pawn shop until they were bought by someone else. I would have liked just one of my nan's swimming trophies, and if I had a time machine then the first place I would visit would be the side of the swimming pool while Nan was steaming through the water, leaving the other swimmers a length or two behind.

The Bryant & May factory never did combust and burn to the ground in minutes, thank God, but the sulphur on the matches they produced must have been bad to inhale because it left my nan with chest problems for the rest of her life, which meant you could always hear her coming before you'd see her.

My nan was so funny and lively that we didn't once complain whenever – every now and then – she would take us to the washhouse with her. With anyone else we would have moaned and thought it was a punishment for some messing around we'd done earlier, but with our nan, the trip was like a little adventure. She would load up with so much laundry that how she got that pram and washing down from the fourth landing of the tenement block had to be a miracle.

Remember, Nan was only five foot tall and stick-thin to

boot but, like a woman possessed, she hung onto that pram like a rodeo cowboy as it dragged and bounced her down every granite step. At the bottom of the steps she would pick our Brian up and sit him on the top of the washing, just in case he ran off – which is what he tended to do, having ants in his pants and always twitching like a hyper bunny – and he sat there on top of that washing, like Lawrence of Arabia on his camel. Nan would then race him and our washing all the way up Parliament Street at top speed, like she was being chased by a wild dog, then right on to Lodge Lane, where the washhouse was at the side entrance to the Lodge Lane swimming baths.

The smell from the washhouse has stayed with me over the years and whenever I smell anything remotely like it, I will stop whatever it is I'm doing and just breathe it in, and I'm back there outside that washhouse, with me and our Brian playing in the street with the empty pram. Rallying up and down, taking turns to push each other while waiting for our lovely Nan to reappear and load up the pram with carbolic-scented washing. By the time she did come out, we would both be knackered from playing, but Brian was the one who got to ride the clean bundle of washing all the way back.

Home, and Nan would start making dinner; this was usually Scouse. Nan made the best Scouse in the whole of Liverpool city. And although hers was the only Scouse I'd properly tasted, I knew it just had to be the best because even the neighbours used to comment on it, and lots of them knew whenever my nan was making Scouse as they would just happen by for a chat when there was a panful on the stove. Nan was always generous, but not stupid. She had a family of her own to feed, so she would give the visitor a small bowl and then see them off.

I did enjoy my nan's Scouse, but it wasn't my favourite meal. I, like most kids, used to come home from school hoping to see a big plate of egg and chips, or sausage and chips, or anything else as long as it was parked next to chips. But Nan's Scouse was always a welcome runner-up.

Now, the reason I'm rattling on about Scouse is that I recently spotted a magazine article with a recipe for that most traditional meal of us Liverpudlians, the ingredients of which were as follows: 1 pound of beef, 1 pound of lamb, onions, carrots, potatoes, stock cubes, vegetable oil, Worcestershire sauce, salt, pepper and water. Out of the eleven ingredients on this list, my nan's scouse contained six, and not one of them began with 'one pound of…'

Although Nan couldn't afford pounds of beef and lamb and would have to make do with whatever meat leftovers there were, she always used the greenest greens and the most orange carrots and always made sure the potatoes were firm and without lots of eyes because, to be honest, most of the Scouse was to be made up of potatoes anyway so they had to be good quality. Other people used Scouse as an excuse for mashing together any wilting veg and meat on the turn just to make a cheap evening meal. But Nan had much too much pride to be passing off rotten food as a bowl of Scouse. I remember seeing greyish, pale versions of the dish at friends' houses and quickly turning down offers of, 'Would you like a bowl of Scouse,

Christine?' Nah, my Nan was of that age-old tradition: 'If something's worth doing, it's worth doing right'.

One of Nan's favourite television programmes was the American Western series, *Bonanza*. She would get all of her chores out of the way – with the exception of ironing, which she could do while watching telly – and sit down with a cuppa and me and watch the episode in silence. What with Jim Reeves and *Bonanza*, I think she had a secret little thing going on with all things American. I'll never forget one Sunday, about an hour before *Bonanza* was due to start, Nan got up from the couch and said she was feeling tired.

'I'm just going to have a little sleep, Christine,' she said. 'Make sure you wake me up when *Bonanza* starts.'

I remember she ruffled my hair as she walked past me on her way to the bedroom. I didn't think anything was wrong because I was a kid and was already engrossed in what was on the telly but, an hour later, when Grandad went to wake her up, he couldn't.

'Christine, go and fetch Mrs Dennis!' he shouted.

Mrs Dennis was our next-door neighbour and wasn't a qualified doctor or anything, but I think my grandad was just so panicked, he needed another adult to tell him what was happening. Mrs Dennis couldn't wake Nan either, so she told me to fetch my mam. Even with all the panic that was going on at that moment, I just wasn't seeing why everyone was fussing. I remember sulking as I went to get Mam because I was convinced I was going to miss *Bonanza*.

Within minutes an ambulance arrived, sirens blasting

throughout the tenements, and the two medics managed to wake Nan up. She looked bewildered: 'I just want to sleep,' she said, almost in a daze. In what seemed like seconds the ambulance men had hurried Nan on to a stretcher and were ready to take her to the hospital. They asked who was going to accompany her and Mam immediately reached for my hand: 'We'll go, Christine, we'll look after her, won't we?'

I nodded, only too pleased to be getting a ride in an ambulance.

I was so excited; I'd never been in an ambulance before. I knew a friend who had been and he'd said that they drive as fast as lightning and don't stop for anything, and if anything does get in the way, the ambulance just goes straight through it. So, I was really hoping something got in the way. Inside the ambulance, I was much more interested in looking out of the tinted windows than noticing what was going on with Nan. And when the ambulance arrived at the hospital and the doors opened to medical staff rushing around everywhere, I felt so important because I knew that all that fuss was for Nan.

In the corridor we were met by a doctor, who walked alongside Nan's trolley all the way to the ward, through what seemed like miles and miles of sterile white corridors. By now, she had fallen asleep again.

The doctor drew the curtains around her bed and I was sent outside. He examined her for what seemed like hours, but eventually a nurse came to get me and I was let back in to see her. Nan's bed was the only part of the ward with a light and as the nurse pulled back the curtain, I was so relieved to

SCOUSE, CHOPPERS & SPACE HOPPERS

see my nan sitting up in bed, drinking a cup of tea. 'Do you want some tea, Christine?' she said, but I just shook my head and smiled at her.

I remember Mam's face was so worried and she looked worn and much paler than Nan even. We were only allowed to say a quick goodnight and then the nurse said we would have to go, so my nan could rest. I reached up to give her a kiss and she stroked my head.

'You be a good girl,' she said. 'I'll see you tomorrow, Christine.'

Mam kissed and hugged her, and I could see she was trying her hardest to hold back tears. We went to walk away and my nan said, 'Christine, I haven't got me glasses, so when you get home, put them in your coat pocket and you can bring them in tomorrow.'

Nan waved as me and Mam held hands and walked out of the ward. I remember wondering what all the fuss had been about. *She's just a little tired*, I thought to myself on the way home, wondering why they'd brought her into hospital just for that; to sit up in bed with a cup of tea?

That was the last time I saw my nan. The following day, I put her glasses in my pocket as I prepared for a visit to the hospital that would never happen.

My lovely Nan had died and gone to heaven in the early hours of the morning.

* * *

Recently, I was watching a programme on TV called *Britain's Worst Weather* and it brought back memories from the early seventies where a massive thunderstorm took place that went on all night long and scared my mam into thinking it could be the end of the world.

Mam had ushered us under the bed as the flashes of lightning lit up the room and the thunder shook the house. A horrendous night, it seemed to go on forever. Before we got under the bed, she made us count, as she always did in thunderstorms, after every bang of the thunder: one, one-thousand! Two, two-thousand! But this storm was ridiculously loud so she must have thought, to hell with this, and shoved us under the bed instead.

The reason I'm mentioning this storm is because Nan was terrified of thunderstorms, and even after she had left us, my mam would put her ashes in a cupboard away from the thunder and lightning as though she was still with us. She would also turn off the telly and unplug the plugs in case we got struck by the lighting, because that's what Nan used to do. At that time families kept the ashes of loved ones in the house rather than burying them. It was tradition and a way to keep their presence alive. Most of us at some time would talk to the urn the same way you might visit a loved-one's grave and have a full-on conversation.

Another thing Mam used to do, like my nan before her, was move any knives and forks from near the front or back doors and then open the doors to let the lightning pass through the house. Sometimes in a normal lightning storm, she would tell me to fetch my nan's ashes off the window ledge in case 'she gets struck by a fork of lighting'. At which point, Dad would call her a silly mare and say, 'Margie, the bloody urn's made of plastic!'

***

Thank you, my beautiful Nan, for spending my childhood helping to raise me, and for supporting my mam and dad, and although you only had an old radiogram, an overly polished front door step, a solitary gold tooth, and a thin wedding band to your name when you left us, you took with you a wealth of love and happy memories worth more than all the riches of the earth.

Christine xxx

CHAPTER THIRTY-TWO

THEY CALL HIM FLIPPER

This chapter has one purpose only, and that's to show you how odd and completely random the Liverpool of the sixties and seventies really was, so I hope you haven't fallen asleep by now because you'll need to keep up. Firstly, what I'm about to recall doesn't even sound like it happened at all, at least that's what friends tell me when I try relating the story to them. Cast your mind back to the mid-1960s, to a TV show called *Flipper*.

Flipper was a dolphin who – like Lassie the dog and Skippy the bush kangaroo – always came to the rescue of anyone who found themselves up shit creek. The series was really popular, but only ran from 1964–67, as by 1967, they had totally exhausted the amount of adventures a heroic bottlenose dolphin could have. At the time I watched the show because I'd seen a very young and very fit Burt Reynolds in one of the first episodes and, as with most things, having seen them once, I was hooked.

Now, sometime between the final series and 1969, the Flipper owners decided to take Flipper and a number of other dolphins on an around-the-world tour. The part of this story that my friends never believe is that the tour came to Liverpool: to Garston swimming baths, to be exact. I kid you not, honest to God; cross my heart and hope to die. Garston swimming baths had the biggest swimming pool of any swimming baths in Liverpool at that time, and for some unknown reason, the Garston swimming bath committee decided that having a load of world-famous dolphins turn up and put on a show was the thing to do. Honestly, I shit you not, these dolphins really did turn up and, what's more, Mo, the girl I hung around with at the time, had a spare ticket to see the show.

Mo's mum had been copping for one of the guys who had something to do with the committee and he'd given her five tickets, one for her, her friend, and her three kids – forgetting she actually only had two kids. So I was invited as long as I could make my own way to Garston and back. This wasn't a problem as my Aunty Sally lived in Speke, which wasn't far from Garston at all. And if it was to see Flipper, I'd have bloody well walked there if I had to! Sally's husband, Uncle Tommy, grew rhubarb on a local allotment and always used to supply us with the best of the crop in return for some of the pies my mam used to make with it. We'd always go there on the 86 bus so we could get the rhubarb and go see the airplanes at Speke airport flying overhead; so travelling to see the dolphins in Garston wouldn't be a problem.

When the big day came and my mam handed me the bus fare, I was off to Garston like a shot. Mo, her sister, her mum, and her mum's friend met me outside the swimming baths. I'd spotted them as my bus was pulling up to the stop opposite the swimming baths. They were stood in the centre of a long queue of really excited kids and parents. Some of the kids had made banners to hold up, which had drawings and cut-outs of Flipper and the cast of the show. I thought the banners were a bit over the top and you could tell that the kids' parents had made them because they were way too good, but whoever made them didn't matter when these kids and their banner-making parents were suddenly called forward and let in before anyone else, which was as friggin' unfair as you could get in my opinion, but no one else seemed to be complaining so I shut my face.

Inside the baths it felt strange because there wasn't the usual smell of bleach that you used to get in swimming baths. Mo's mum explained to us that they didn't use bleach when the dolphins were there in case they got ill from swallowing the water. So, in other words, they had dolphin Health and Safety, but no human Health and Safety, nice!

We sat in the seats that surrounded the giant swimming pool and stared down at the covers that kept the dolphins from our view. Then the music started and the announcer began his spiel, 'Ladies and gentlemen, boys and girls, and all *Coryphaena hippurus...*' the announcer grinned as the audience looked puzzled. 'That's the Latin name for Flipper and his friends!' The crowd went crazy and started screaming as the dolphins swam into view and darted across the swimming pool. The dolphins that started the show were amazing, leaping out of the water and splashing everyone as they went back in. 'There's Flipper!' I shouted, as a sectioned-off part of the pool was suddenly revealed to show the aquatic icon. I really couldn't believe my eyes that the dolphin I'd seen so many times on TV was right in front of me, doing amazing tricks and making its signature dolphin clicking sound, just like it did on the telly.

They say you should never meet your heroes as they might disappoint. Well, Flipper didn't disappoint at all, in fact, he actually went a little too far to impress in my opinion. The fella who was encouraging the dolphins to flip and perform suddenly called out for three volunteers, who would get to feed the dolphins. Mo put her hand up, so I did too. The fella called me and Mo and one boy over to the poolside and lined us up. I was first in the line.

'Now, little girl,' the fella said to me in an American accent that I thought was super-cool, 'what you do is you hold the fish out between your finger and thumb and Flipper will let you feed him.' He then gave me a dead fish that felt cold and gross, and I had to hold it over the pool. I looked back and laughed nervously at Mo just as Flipper flew up out of the water and snatched the fish from my hand. I totally shit myself and screamed because, as I turned back, Flipper was just taking the fish from my hand and he was shiny and massive and as in my face as he could get without actually headbutting me! I jumped backwards and started crying like a little tit.

When I saw Mo pissing herself laughing, I stopped crying and tried to look like I'd enjoyed the whole experience, but nobody believed me, just as nobody believed me for the years that followed whenever I told the story of Flipper's visit to Garston swimming baths. If there's anybody still doubting my story, then all I can say is thank God for Google!

CHAPTER THIRTY-THREE

THE (ALMOST) LEAVING OF LIVERPOOL

Sixties and seventies Liverpool was my home and all I knew. It was exciting, it was the music centre of the world, and – did I mention? – it was my home! So how scary was it when in the mid- to late 1960s, Dad suddenly announced that we might be moving to Australia. At the time, there was a scheme that had been running since shortly after the Second World War that was aimed at repopulating Australia and supplying workers for its thriving factories and businesses. It was called the Assisted Passage Migration Scheme and was nicknamed by Australians as The Ten Pound Poms, because £10 was all you had to pay to migrate to Australia and the Aussie government would pay the rest.

My dad had been forced to go on strike when he worked for the Ford Motor Company back then, and I remember him coming home all disgruntled and looking downtrodden. Mam was really concerned because he wasn't the kind of person that let things get to him. Then he suddenly came out with it and said to her, 'Margie, do you fancy seeing Australia?' and she said, 'What cinema's it on?' It turned out that it wasn't the title of a film at all, my dad was basically saying, 'Should we move to Australia?' He wanted to get away from strikes and having no money, and wanted a new beginning, a new life Down Under.

Dad explained that Ford were going to keep pissing off the unions and they were going to keep retaliating by calling strikes, and while the leaders of the unions and the managers of Ford were sitting back in their fancy houses while all this crap was going on, the simple workers were bearing the brunt of it all and having to almost starve, along with their families. He then went on telling my mam all about how amazing Australia was and how lots of the guys he knew from work had already upped and left for a life in the sun as far from Liverpool as you could get without actually leaving the planet.

Mam was silent as she listened to my dad pleading his case for pissing off out of Liverpool. I'd overheard his opening sentence and was in two minds as to whether I'd want to leave. I hated school because all the teachers were dickheads, who always made fun of me and picked on me whenever they got the urge. I had good friends, but I could make new Australian friends quite easily. I would be considered different in Australia and all the kids would probably want to get to know me and hang around with me, which meant I would probably have lots of boyfriends. And The Bee Gees were from Australia so it must be a good place to live because they always looked happy and had the biggest toothy smiles in history. As you can tell, my logic at that time was all over the fuckin' place!

The more my dad talked, the more convinced I was that we were leaving to go and live in the land of The Bee Gees, Skippy, koalas and didgeridoos. He made it sound like the most exciting place on earth, and he said that we would have lots of land; land that was right near the coast so we could visit the beach every other day. Then he said that we might even be able to live on a beach because the coast of Australia was so big, practically everyone could live on the beaches. I think he was talking for a half-hour and all this time my mam was nodding and I was grinning like an idiot.

He finally took a breath while Mam paused for a moment, like she was thinking about, and actually considering, everything he'd said. She then turned and said, 'I'm not friggin' going to Australia! I don't even know where it is!' Dad was a little bit taken aback because he thought her silence meant that he'd talked her round. 'It's the other side of the world!' he said. Mam stood up from the chair and said, 'Well, you can get lost, coz I'm not going!' and she walked out of the room and that was the end of my dad's Aussie dream.

I don't know what would have happened if we had gone to Australia but, with hindsight, I'm really glad we never bothered. There was no way Australia could be better than Liverpool at that time, even if it did have beaches, koalas, kangaroos and The Bee Gees. Liverpool was the most happening place there was, not Australia. We had New Brighton Beach and Wales. We had unique weather that produced sun, rain, wind, warmth and cold, all in the same day. And the Aussies didn't have snow, or even slush, so my mam's home-stitched balaclavas would be redundant if we did emigrate.

Also, I'd heard that the Aussies were all tall and good-looking, so I would – in reality – have had an even harder time finding a boyfriend there than I was having here. And they didn't have football in Australia either; they had Aussie rules football, which was totally fucked up and nothing like the real football our Liverpool and Everton teams played so well. This would mean that Mam and Dad wouldn't be able to go to the match when they wanted. And who knows what I'd have become, if I'd gone to Australia? I might never have got into show business because I would never have gone for the Ken Dodd Diddy Men audition. And if I had got into show business in Australia, I might have ended up in *Neighbours* or *Home and A-fuckin'-way*! God, take me now!

Nah, the Liverpool of the sixties and seventies was most definitely a keeper and I wouldn't swap Scouse memories for Aussie memories, not for all the tea in China. The Liverpool back then prepared me for what life had to offer. It gave me a platform to start my career. It gave me idols that I was proud to call fellow Scousers. It gave me knocks, along with pats on the back. And it surrounded me with the most colourful experiences a kid could hope to experience. I loved Liverpool then, and I love it even more now because…

> We speak with an accent exceedingly rare,
> Meet under a statue exceedingly bare,
> And if you want a cathedral, we've got one to spare
> In my Liverpool home.

PETER MCGOVERN, *songwriter, activist, Scouser*

ACKNOWLEDGEMENTS

Firstly, thank you to Margie. Where do I begin about our friendship? Well, let's go back thirty-six years, when we were skint, became neighbours, and then went on to become best friends. People always take us for sisters – oh my God! We must have morphed into each other.

So this dedication is for the times you've been there for me (especially when helping to jog my memory while writing this book), the endless cups of coffee, for all those times when you've had to be my English teacher, telling me how to spell this, that, and the other. . . Have you got a pen?

For everything we've been through together; the laughter and the tears. Without your friendship my life would have been so empty.

Next, this book probably would never have been written without a chance meeting I had with Vinny Cleghorne.

I wanted to write a children's book and was looking for an illustrator. Hayley, my daughter, told me all about Vinny, a fabulous artist and writer she was friends with on Facebook. We got in touch by phone and whilst talking pictures he fed me the seed to write a book about growing up in Liverpool. Once we got together he breathed life into my words and the book was done. We have since gone on to write a comedy TV series. Thank you, Vinny, for your knowledge and guidance and may we go on to greater things.

To my childhood friends from the past, who played out our dreams amongst the derelict wastelands of sixties and seventies Liverpool 8. I hope you found your dreams.

My brothers Brian, Ian, David and Jay for helping shape me into the person I am today; the sibling bond we have is unbreakable.

And Alan Haigh, my dearest friend, who has been like a brother to me. Thank you for your support and friendship over the years.

My daughters Tracy and Hayley who keep me on my toes and also at the ATM. . . Love you really.

My granddaughters who have grown and blossomed into beautiful young women – I wish you every happiness in your life.

For Leah Bell, who turned me back into a working actress through the play *Dirty Dusting*. We have become great friends co-writing the successful comedy play *Seriously Dead*. Leah, for your friendship, kindness and taking me under your wing, allowing me to become an extended part of your family and the flower in your attic. Trust you to get a dandelion! I can't thank you enough.

I couldn't end this without a special mention to my beautiful partner Julian. You loved me even though I was broken. Your warmth and patience put me back together again.

You never fail to make me feel complete and especially loved. I love you forever.

PS. Margie, put the sick bucket down.

CO-AUTHOR'S NOTE

I was first introduced to Crissy Rock as an artist rather than a writer, when an opportunity arose to illustrate a children's picture book that Crissy had in the pipeline. When we discussed the illustrations, the conversation slowly turned from picture books to novels and we found that we had many things in common, including comedy writing and growing up in Toxteth, Liverpool. Within an hour, Crissy had asked me to work with her on a new book she'd been considering writing. I said yes, but only if she was happy to proceed after working together on the first chapter. . . She was happy.

Crissy and I have since written a new comedy/drama television series, *The Tungsten Flyers*, and we have a string of future projects planned.

It has been a delight working with Crissy as she is one of the loveliest, most creative and genuine people I've ever met.

CRISSY ROCK is a Liverpool-born comedian and actress, best known for her major role in hit ITV comedy show *Benidorm*. A gifted story-teller, her one-woman shows and live comedy have met with critical acclaim. Described by the *Liverpool Echo* as 'a Liverpool legend', Crissy had an eventful childhood growing up one of Britain's storied and iconic cities. This is Crissy's second book, following her bestselling autobiography, *This Heart Within Me Burns*.

VINCE CLEGHORNE has been a film director, cartoonist, dance teacher, BBC playwright and screenwriter. He has written award-winning screenplays, novels and children's books, and has an extensive design record undertaking commissions from Sony, English Heritage and the Tate Gallery. But his finest moments were becoming a dad to his son, Kyle, and a granddad to his granddaughter, Amber. At present he lives in Liverpool's Georgian Quarter, with a very spoilt cat and a wealth of possibilities. Assisting Crissy with the writing of this book has been one of his most enjoyable projects to date.